EATYMOLOGY

the dictionary of modern gastronomy

JOSH FRIEDLAND

 sourcebooks

Published by Sourcebooks, Inc.
P.O. Box 4410, Naperville, Illinois 60567-4410
(630) 961-3900
Fax: (630) 961-2168
www.sourcebooks.com

Library of Congress Cataloging-in-Publication Data

Friedland, Josh.
  The dictionary of modern gastronomy / Josh Friedland.
    pages cm
  Includes bibliographical references.
  (hardcover : alk. paper) 1. Gastronomy—Dictionaries. I. Title.
  TX631.F75 2015
  641.01'3003—dc23
                      2015021941

Printed and bound in the United States of America.

VP 10 9 8 7 6 5 4 3 2 1

For Anya and Asher

CONTENTS

SOURCES

ACKNOWLEDGMENTS

ABOUT THE AUTHOR

INTRODUCTION

Throughout human history, food has served as one of the great engines of linguistic invention and reinvention. Hundreds of thousands of years may have passed between an early hominid's first grunt over a handful of tasty nuts and the glowing 140-character review of ramen you just read on Twitter ("#amazeballs"), but the instinct to put words to food is the same. Every time we eat something new and discover novel tastes, smells, and textures, we feel compelled to find words to describe our experiences. Tracing the origins of language, historian Simon Schama cites the first meals of infancy: "If our defining characteristic is indeed as language animal, the lingo compulsion does actually get underway with mother's milk; that as soon as we eat, we feel the need to make some noise about it, a sound that will end up as verbalisation and, eventually, writing."

The history of food and language could easily fill a thousand pages. This slim volume looks at just a sliver of our most recent past, gleaning one hundred newly coined words from the world of modern gastronomy. Nearly all of the entries have been invented since the turn of the twenty-first century, a boom time for the celebration of all things culinary when food got big and, let's face it, a little weird. The rise of the rock star chef, hard-core locavorism, social media junkies, food fetishism, pastry mash-ups, and environmental dread have spawned a brand-new vocabulary to capture our wild and woolly new gastronomic reality.

As I came across these fascinating (and often hilarious) new words for eating, drinking, and thinking about food, I found myself driven to track down more. Eventually, this burgeoning collection turned into *Eatymology*.

My hope is that this book will serve as a snapshot of some of the excesses of the current food scene and also a window into some of its more curious corners. Entries like *brogurt* (coined by journalists to describe yogurt targeted at men) demonstrate the absurd lengths that the food industry will go to in order to reach consumers in a very competitive marketplace. *Selmelier* (salt sommelier—yes, there are enough kinds of salt in the world to justify their existence), *brocavore* (male hipster gastronomes), and *raota* (ramen nerds) reflect the current demographics of food folk: diverse, niche, and extremely obsessive about everything they put in their mouths. It's not just the food industry that's caught this word fever either. From academia and science come strange new terms such as *carnism* (the ideology that supports eating meat) and *food swamp* (the inundation of poor neighborhoods with high-calorie foods), which attempt to grapple with the complicated food choices we face today and their larger impact on our bodies and the environment around us. Even the onset of global warming and the complicated relationship between food and the environment has spawned such fascinating new phrases as *food bubble*, *virtual water*, and *bluewashing*. As silly or strange as these may sound, they echo a very serious and growing concern about knowing where our food comes from and how it's gotten to our plates. For all its pleasures, modern food can have an ugly underbelly, and neologisms like *blood cashews* (nuts processed under abusive conditions) and *honey laundering* (illegal trade in tainted honey) speak to the inherent dangers of globalization.

It's not all doom and gloom, however. New words can be great fun, and many of the ones collected here were chosen for their unusual character and quirkiness, not to mention their irresistible humor. A term like *barista wrist* (a café-induced injury caused by the repetitive motion of making too many coffee drinks) might cause you to crack a smile. Some, like *duckeasy* (an underground foie gras supper club) or *felfie* (a farmer selfie, naturally), may even trigger a belly laugh. Others are wonderfully literary, such as *white whale*, an artful term for those rare beers that elude ale aficionados just as Moby Dick dodged Ahab.

As you'll see, the entries take on many different shapes and forms. Some are portmanteau words that blend two words (or parts of words) into one. Others have been formed through affixation, where an old word has been cannibalized to communicate something new. Still more are loanwords that we've borrowed from foreign languages and assimilated into our everyday English. While many of the words collected in *Eatymology* have become part of the food lexicon, a number are what linguists call "nonce words," coinages invented for a one-time use or a special occasion.

As odd as some of the terms may seem (I'm looking at you, *gastrosexual*), I can assure you that they are all entirely real and sourced from articles, books, film, and online media. Each entry includes a definition of the food word or phrase, information about its origins (wherever possible, as I was unable to locate exact origins for some of the words), and other interesting historical tidbits, related synonyms and homonyms, and cultural flotsam and jetsam. If these bite-sized entries haven't satisfied you, check out the sources at the end of the book for a complete bibliographic record and further reading on each entry.

What will happen next for these delicious neologisms? Are they destined to go the way of *hollow-meat*, *phrygology*, and *numbles*—obsolete words for poultry, the art of frying, and deer offal—that have disappeared from modern speech? Or will future generations be *bone luging*, hoarding bacon for the *aporkalypse*, and complaining about *Cronut*-eating *foodiots* well into the twenty-second century? Only time will tell as we keep swallowing up new culinary experiences and fattening ourselves with novel ways to describe them.

100
◦ NEW WORDS ◦
about FOOD

A•PORK•A•LYPSE (*noun*):

A calamitous event involving a precipitous decline in the supply of pork.

≡ ORIGINS ≡

Fears of a worldwide shortage of bacon in 2013, dubbed the *aporkalypse*, exploded in social media following the dissemination of a 2012 report by the UK's National Pig Association, which claimed that heavy drought conditions in Europe had so damaged corn and soybean feed crops that a sharp reduction of pork production was inevitable. The hysteria appeared to be unfounded, as the global pig supply actually increased from 970 million animals to 977 million in 2013, according to the Food and Agriculture Organization of the United Nations. Nevertheless, bacon lovers live in fear that this could actually become their reality one day.

≡ PREHISTORY ≡

The word *aporkalypse* (and synonyms *parmageddon* and *snoutbreak*) had a brief appearance in 2009 as a buzzword for the panic over the worldwide swine flu pandemic.

≡ SOME OTHER APORKALYPSES ≡

The "Aporkalypse" is the name for an annual stunt launched in 2012 on the Sportsman Channel's *Pigman* series, where hunter and host Brian "Pigman" Quaca launches a helicopter assault on feral pigs. Aporkalypse is also the name for a sweet and savory bacon and chocolate porter created by the Brains brewery in Wales, and Aporkalypse Now is an oatmeal bacon stout sold by the Hogsback Brewing Company in Ottawa, Canada. Either beer might pair nicely with an Aporkalypse breakfast sandwich, launched in 2014 in Ontario, Canada, by the fast-food chain Carl's Jr. It contains egg, cheese, and a trifecta of pork products: sausage, bacon, and ham.

A·RU·GU·LANCE (*noun*):

A perceived attitude of superiority and snobbery manifested in a predilection for pricey—yet delicious—peppery greens.

....

= ORIGINS =

Arugula has come a long way from its humble roots as a weed in the Mediterranean to its status as a symbol of food snobbery in the United States. One of the earliest references to the word *arugulance*, a blend of *arugula* and *arrogance*, appeared in 2007 when conservative blogger Michael Bates chastised then-presidential candidate Barack Obama for his "typical liberal arugulance" at a Democratic primary campaign stop. "Anybody gone into Whole Foods lately and see what they charge for arugula?" Obama had asked a crowd in Adel, Iowa. "I mean, they're charging a lot of money for this stuff."

Arugulance got further traction in the media following a 2009 *New York Times* op-ed article by columnist Maureen Dowd profiling the renowned chef and food advocate Alice Waters. Defending herself against charges of elitism, Waters told Dowd, "I'm just put into that arugulance place. I own a fancy restaurant. I own an expensive restaurant. I never thought of it as fancy. People don't know we're supporting 85 farms and ranches and all of that."

≡ HISTORY ≡

The *Oxford English Dictionary* dates the first appearance of the word *arugula* in American English to a 1960 *New York Times* article by food editor Craig Claiborne on the culinary charms of the green and its many names (rucola, rocket, roquette, etc.). "The phrase 'secret ingredient' is a slightly ludicrous thing since it conjures up images of Mephisphelean brews," wrote Claiborne. "Most Italian chefs know, however, that arugula or rocket—call it what you will—is the secret ingredient of many of the salads-about-town."

≡ LUSCIOUS LEAVES ≡

Centuries before arugula made its way from peasant dish to bludgeon wielded in the class wars, it had an ancient reputation as an aphrodisiac. "Moretum," a poem ascribed to Virgil, contains a reference to *eruca*, the Latin name for arugula, in the line "*et veneris revocans eruca morantuem*" ("the rocket excites the sexual desire of drowsy people"). Think about that the next time you stroll the produce aisle at Whole Foods.

BA•RIS•TA WRIST

(*noun*): A painful condition afflicting some coffee workers as a result of repetitive motions involved in making coffee drinks.

≡ THE DAILY GRIND ≡

A survey of 475 coffee workers by the website Sprudge.com found that 47 percent of those surveyed had experienced upper-body repetitive stress injuries that they attributed to their jobs. In addition, 20 percent had experienced heart palpitations or chest pains, and 62 percent believed "their job or caffeine intake had caused emotional problems such as mood variability, depression, or trouble interacting emotionally with others." Samantha Lino, a former Starbucks barista, told the *New York Post* in 2014 that her doctor recommended she leave her job because she was suffering from medial epicondylitis (also known as golfer's elbow) "caused in this case by the repetitive stress of lifting heavy pitchers of milk and making multistep drinks in complicated machines."

≡ PREVENTION ≡

To avoid injuries while tamping coffee grounds to make espresso, some coffee shops teach their employees stretching techniques to avoid injury, employ yoga instructors to train employees in better posture, and alter counter height to improve the ergonomics of making drinks.

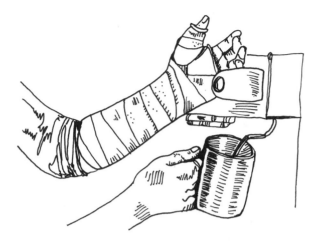

"My doc said surgery for carpal tunnel is pointless. I essentially had to let my body heal, which meant that I had to quit being a barista. Now I sit behind a desk and I wish every day to be out with my customers, exploring the coffee world, and seeing farms! But those jobs are so hard to find without being forced to deal with torn ligaments."

—ANONYMOUS BARISTA

BEER MILE (*noun*): An athletic competition in which runners must run one mile while consuming four beers. Vomiting is penalized.

....

≡ ORIGINS ≡

According to a 2014 article in *Runner's World*, the first beer mile competition took place in August 1989 when seven runners in their late teens and early twenties came together at Burlington Central High School in Burlington, Ontario, to chug and race their way around the track. Since the 1990s, Beermile.com, an online clearinghouse for suds-fueled contests, has logged more than ninety thousand entries and five thousand races in its database.

≡ CHUGGING COMPETITION ≡

At the inaugural Beer Mile World Championships held on December 3, 2014, in Austin, Texas, Corey Gallagher, a twenty-seven-year-old Canadian mail carrier, won the men's title with a time of 5:00.23. Beth Herndon, a twenty-nine-year-old environmental geochemist from Fort Wayne, Indiana, was the top finisher in the women's division with a world record time of 6:17.76.

≡ VARIATIONS ≡

The Queen's Chunder Mile: Competitors must drink one twenty-ounce imperial pint of beer every quarter mile for one mile (vomiting allowed).

Clydesdale Division: A standard beer mile, but runners must be thirty-five years or older and weigh at least two hundred pounds.

The 3000 m Vodka Steeplechase: Runners must consume seven shots of vodka while completing a standard three-kilometer steeplechase race.

4 × 40 Beer Relay: A team event involving four runners per team. Each must drink one forty-ounce beer and run a quarter mile.

The Beer Half Marathon: Competitors must drink thirteen beers while running thirteen miles.

BEST•O•VORE (*noun*): One who eats foods they deem to be the best in taste and quality whenever possible, regardless of their geographical origin.

....

≡ ORIGINS ≡

Bestovore (alternate spelling *bestavore*) was coined by food writer and former *New York Times* restaurant critic Mimi Sheraton, who described her philosophy of eating in an interview with the food blog Eater.com: "If it tastes good, then that's fine. I'm not a total locavore. I'll say that. I consider myself a bestovore. Never mind local if it is not the best. But if I were faced with a Pennsylvania peach or Georgia peach, I would take the Georgia peach every time and let them sort it out in Pennsylvania."

≡ ANTONYM ≡

The opposite of a bestovore is a *locavore*, one who limits their consumption to foods grown locally. *Locavore* was the *New Oxford American Dictionary* 2007 "Word of the Year."

≡ GLOCAL CUISINE ≡

Somewhere between the extremes of locavorism and bestovorism lies "glocal" cuisine, defined by the *Globe and Mail* in 2010 as cooking that blends international recipes with local ingredients: "In Canadian restaurants, chefs are matching food traditions from other countries with ingredients from nearby producers to create a new made-in-Canada global-local cuisine. Call it 'glocal.'"

"As someone with a love for the exotic (being of Scottish and Maori descent, raised in coastal New Zealand and trained in one of the worlds [sic] best culinary centres—Melbourne) the thought of having to create and produce food that stays close to my roots (whatever they are) would be like telling a painter not to use blue or red."

—PETER GORDON, BRITISH CHEF AND BESTOVORE

BIS·TRON·O·MY (*noun*):

A Parisian restaurant trend toward reenvisioning bistros as places where creative chefs serve reinvented classic dishes at affordable prices.

═ ORIGINS ═

The term evolved from *bistronomique* (a combination of *bistro* and *gastronomique*), coined by French journalist Sébastien Demorand, which morphed into *bistronomie* and is now anglicized as *bistronomy*. It was the title of a 2007 article by food writer and editor Christine Muhlke on the French food trend in the *New York Times Magazine*. French chef Yves Camdeborde is considered to be the father of the bistronomy movement, starting the trend in 1992 when he opened his Paris restaurant La Régalade serving high-end prix-fixe menus at low prices.

═ NEO-BISTROTS ═

Bistronomic restaurants have become known as "néo-bistrots." According to a 2010 *Wall Street Journal* article on the trend, "the defining features of the néo-bistrot appear to be an innovative, cosmopolitan approach, with a refreshingly casual atmosphere and often prix-fixe menus that are priced at less than €50 per person, which passes for cheap in Paris, at least."

═ BISTRONOMY, THE BOOK ═

In 2014, Australian food writer Katrina Meynink published *Bistronomy: French Food Unbound*, compiling one hundred recipes from néo-bistrots around the globe.

"The word bistronomy used to be almost an insult. Pejorative. I'm not a bistrotier monsieur, I'm a chef. What's funny is that this pejorative ring to bistro and attempt to separate us from them has gone the other way. Now the word bistro means quality and good atmosphere, it's astonishing."

—YVES CAMDEBORDE, CHEF AND BISTRONOMY PIONEER

See Also
food·ing (page 82)

BLOOD CASH·EWS

(*noun*): Nuts processed by workers under abusive labor conditions.

≡ ORIGINS ≡

Blood cashews are a play on the term *blood diamonds*, gems mined in war zones and sold to support military causes. The neologism was coined in 2011 by Human Rights Watch (HRW) after it investigated the conditions under which cashews were being processed in Vietnam, the world's largest exporter of the nuts. A report by HRW found that drug users were being punished and detained by the Vietnamese government in "treatment" centers where they were forced to process cashews under abusive and often dangerous conditions. Writing about the abuses for *Global Post*, Joe Amon, director of the health and human rights division at HRW, decried these so-called blood cashews:

"Vietnam advertises itself as a tourist paradise and low-cost hub for manufacturing. But unless the government ends the torture and forced labor of drug users in the name of 'treatment,' it may be equally well known as well as the source of 'blood cashews.'"

≡ BOYCOTT ≡

In 2012, the Coalition to Abolish Modern-day Slavery in Asia called upon consumers worldwide to boycott cashews exported by Vietnam: "The ultimate goal of this boycott campaign against the 'blood cashews' from Vietnam is to free all Vietnamese detainees and prisoners, including political prisoners, from modern-day slavery."

≡ ABUSES ≡

Que Phong, who spent five years in one of the drug treatment centers, was given a daily quota of cashews to husk and peel. According to HRW, "Although the caustic resin from the cashews burnt his hands, he was forced to work for six or seven hours a day. Asked why he performed such hazardous work, he said, 'If you refused to work they slapped you. If you still refused to work then they sent you to the punishment room. Everyone worked.'"

BLUE•WASH•ING (*noun*):
The dissemination of misleading information by food retailers about the environmental bona fides of the fish they sell.

....

≡ ORIGINS ≡

Bluewashing is a corollary to greenwashing, marketing and public relations aimed at distorting the ecological commitment of a corporation. The term was coined in 2010 in an article in the journal *Oryx* on sustainable seafood initiatives. The study noted that in 2002, UK supermarket chain Sainsbury's had committed to sourcing all its wild fish from sustainable sources by 2010. But after working with the Marine Stewardship Council (MSC), a seafood sustainability nonprofit, MSC-certified fish only amount to 1 percent of Sainsbury's total fish sales.

"Just as consumers experienced fatigue in the 1990s after corporate eco-advertising amounted to little action or outcome, so may this decade witness the same fatigue in sustainable seafood campaigns," wrote the authors of the study. "The 'greenwashing' that corporations were accused of in the 1990s could turn into a 'bluewashing' today."

≡ LABELING UNDER FIRE ≡

In 2013, the journal *Biological Conservation* published a study of nineteen formal objections made to the MSC concerning its certification practices since 1997 and concluded that the organization's imprimatur of sustainability "may be misleading both consumers and conservation funders." Reporting on the study, *Nature* noted that it "raises the possibility that the scheme will come to be regarded as 'bluewashing'—analogous to the derogatory term 'greenwashing' leveled at companies that attempt to put a sheen of environmental responsibility on their activities."

≡ HOMONYM ≡

Bluewashing has also been used as a term to critique corporations that seek to burnish their ecological credentials by agreeing to the sustainable, fair labor, and human rights practices of the United Nations Global Compact.

≡ FARMWASHING ≡

In the same way that bluewashing misleads consumers about the ecological provenance of seafood choices, the term *farmwashing* refers to the deployment of idyllic images of farming to create false messages about how food products are made.

BONE BROTH (*noun*):

A stock made from animal bones cooked for an extended period and consumed as a hot beverage.

....

≡ HISTORY ≡

While broth made from animal bones and meat has been around since the prehistoric era, it has gained popularity as a nourishing hot beverage (and coffee replacement) in paleo diet circles. The *New York Times* documented the new trend in a 2015 article: "To those who have taken up 'broth-ing,' it is the content of the bones—including collagen, amino acids, and minerals—that is the source of its health benefits. Extracting the nutrients from bones is accomplished through long cooking and by adding some acid to the pot, like vinegar, wine, or a bit of tomato paste, which loosens and dissolves the tough bits."

≡ BROTH BENEFITS ≡

Advocates of the healing power of bone broth argue that boiling down animal bones, skin, cartilage, tendons, and ligaments into broth will help restore collagen in the body and benefit the musculoskeletal system. Scientists are not convinced. William Percy, an associate professor at the University of South Dakota's Sanford School of Medicine, told NPR, "Since we don't absorb collagen whole, the idea that eating collagen somehow promotes bone growth is just wishful thinking."

≡ STOCK MARKET ≡

In 2014, New York City chef Marco Canora opened Brodo, which serves gourmet "sipping broths" by the cup with add-ins such as ginger juice, Calabrian chili oil, shiitake mushroom tea, freshly grated turmeric, grass-fed bone marrow, beet kvass (fermented beet juice), and organic garlic.

≡ SOUPTAILS ≡

In 2015, Pistola restaurant in Los Angeles introduced "From the Kitchen with Love," a broth cocktail made with six ounces of lamb consommé and two ounces of Glenlivet fifteen-year-old single malt scotch.

BONE LUGE (*noun*): A method of drinking alcohol whereby spirits are poured down a length of hollowed-out roasted marrow bone into one's mouth.

≡ ORIGINS ≡

The bone luge is believed to have originated in 2010 in Portland, Oregon, at the bar Metrovino when bartender Jacob Grier poured a shot of tequila through a roasted cow femur. It is based loosely on "ice luging," a method for pouring a shot of vodka down a "track" made of ice.

HOW TO PERFORM A BONE LUGE

1. Order a cross-cut roasted beef shank bone.

2. Eat the marrow, scrape the bone clean, and press one end to your lips while tipping the other end up.

3. Pour one shot of liquor down the top of the "chute" into your mouth.

4. Document with photos and upload to the Internet via Instagram or your app of choice (hashtag #boneluge, naturally).

≡ PAIRINGS ≡

According to Boneluge.com, the best liquors for luging are fortified wines and aged spirits: "Madeira and sherry are among highly recommended [sic]. The first known documented bone luge was of a reposado tequila, which complemented the savoriness of the marrow. The luge is for top shelf aged spirits, ideally ones your father or grandmother would drink. Bone luging cocktails is largely unexplored territory."

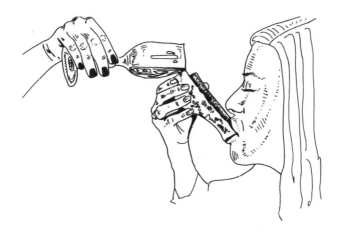

≡ VARIATIONS ≡

Boat Luge: A blend of amaro mixed together in a gravy boat and poured down a marrow bone.

Inverted Luge: Fortified wines mixed with simple syrup, lemon, and crab stock, shaken with ice, and poured down a crab shell.

Crab Leg Luge: Late harvest Riesling poured down a Dungeness crab leg.

BRAT•O•PHO•BIA

(*noun*): An aversion to children dining in restaurants.

....

≡ ORIGINS ≡

The term was coined by the *Economist* magazine in a 2014 article titled "Nippers Not Wanted" on the phenomenon of restaurants and bars that ban children for their unruliness and the resulting backlash by angry parents.

"Bratophobia is not confined to New York. In January Grant Achatz, a Michelin-rated chef, complained about a crying baby in his Chicago restaurant. He could hear it crying even in the noisy kitchen. Via Twitter, he wondered if he should ban children."

≡ BABY BANS ≡

A 2013 report on CNN.com by *Food & Wine* magazine restaurant editor Kate Krader noted a number of restaurants and bars across the United States that had banned children from their establishments:

La Fisheria (Houston, Texas): No children under nine after 7:00 p.m.

McDain's (Monroeville, Pennsylvania): No children under six.

Luigi Q (Hicksville, New York): No children under fourteen.

Grandview Saloon & Coal Hill Steakhouse (Pittsburgh, Pennsylvania): No children under six.

The Sushi Bar (Del Ray, Virginia): No children under eighteen.

≡ GOING VIRAL ≡

In 2014, Chicago chef Grant Achatz of Alinea restaurant launched a debate on Twitter on the ethics of bringing infants to fancy restaurants when he tweeted about a crying baby during dinner service: "Tbl brings 8mo.Old. It cries. Diners mad. Tell ppl no kids? Subject diners 2crying? Ppl take infants 2 plays? Concerts? Hate saying no,but.." Achatz later told *Good Morning America* that restaurateurs are in a difficult position when it comes to kids in their establishments: "We want people to come and enjoy and experience Alinea for what it is. But we also have to be cognizant of the other eighty people that came in to experience Alinea that night."

"Kids shouldn't be running around where people are trying to drink and hook up."

—SOPHIA BLACK, TWENTY-SEVEN, A PATRON OF BROOKLYN BAR THE HOT BIRD, WHICH BANNED CHILDREN IN 2014

BRO·CA·VORE (*noun*):

A male hipster denizen of the local food and restaurant scene.

....

≡ ORIGINS ≡

Food writer and editor Christine Muhlke coined the term in 2010 on the *New York Times T Magazine* blog: "A dude involved in the local food movement and restaurant scene. Typically identified by his fixed-gear bicycle, tattoos, facial hair, and fondness for craft beer (preferably Sixpoint) in a jar, and early Pavement. Commonly seen at Roberta's, Prime Meats, the Bell House."

≡ BROLICIOUS ≡

A web-published project, "Food Diary of a Brocavore," features recipes, photography, and musings by Mike, a self-described brocavore "interested in cooking and the local food movement." Entry 5, a "Green Salad & Mustard Vinaigrette with Windowsill Herbs," includes many of the hallmarks of brocavorism: shallow-focus photographs of a young man outfitted in a red and blue plaid shirt snipping homegrown mesclun and herbs, mixing his salad by hand, and enjoying his meal while reading the *New Yorker* accompanied by wine poured into a mason jar.

≡ BROCONUNDRUM ≡

Episode 196 of John Hodgman's *Judge John Hodgman* podcast, titled "Brocavore," involved a dispute between two brothers who pledged to only eat food they had grown and raised for one year but argued over whether there could be room for a few exceptions. Hodgman ruled in favor of making everyday allowances for salt, pepper, and vitamins and once-per-year exceptions for Fresca, wine, chocolate, coffee, Moxie, instant ramen noodles, shredded soy cheese, Duck Dynasty beef jerky, Kraft macaroni and cheese, Habbersett scrapple, gin, Cheez Waffies, and bananas.

≡ GOING BROCAL ≡

The best places to find brocavores, according to Christine Muhlke:

- Pricing cleverly named sausage at the vegan-owned butcher shop
- Fingering axes at the Best Made Company store (36 White Street, New York, New York)
- Portland, Oregon; Oakland, California; Brooklyn, New York; Asheville, North Carolina; Nashville, Tennessee
- Any restaurant, coffee bar, or bar with "& co." in the name
- Buying a fermentation crock at the local "mercantile"

BROC·CO·LI MAN·DATE (*noun*):

A hypothetical government requirement that citizens buy broccoli.

....

≡ ORIGINS ≡

During oral arguments on the Affordable Care Act in 2012, Supreme Court Justice Antonin Scalia famously invoked the concept of the "broccoli mandate" as a straw man to dispute the constitutionality of the insurance mandate in the health care law. "Everybody has to buy food sooner or later," Scalia argued. "Therefore, you can make people buy broccoli."

≡ PRECEDENTS ≡

In 2010, two years before the Supreme Court case, Senator Tom Coburn asked Associate Justice Elena Kagan during her confirmation hearings about a hypothetical law requiring the consumption of fruits and vegetables: "If I wanted to sponsor a bill and it said, 'Americans, you have to eat three vegetables and three fruits every day,' and I got it through Congress and it's now the law of the land, got to do it, does that violate the commerce clause?" "Sounds like a dumb law," replied Kagan.

Terence P. Jeffrey, the editor in chief of CNS News (formerly known as the Conservative News Service) is credited by the *New York Times* with the first public mention of broccoli in the context of the commerce clause of the Constitution in his 2009 article "Can Obama and Congress Order You to Buy Broccoli?"

≡ BRASSICAPHOBIA ≡

President George H. W. Bush may be responsible for originally demonizing broccoli among conservatives with disparaging remarks he made about the brassica in 1990. "I do not like broccoli," President Bush said, responding to questions about a broccoli ban he had imposed aboard Air Force One. "And I haven't liked it since I was a little kid and my mother made me eat it. And I'm president of the United States, and I'm not going to eat any more broccoli!"

BRO·GURT (*noun*): Yogurt marketed to men with messages touting gender-based health and nutrition benefits.

≡ ORIGINS ≡

New York magazine's blog *Grub Street* coined the term to describe Powerful Yogurt, a high-protein Greek yogurt launched in March 2013 and targeted at men. The company touted the masculine bona fides of its product: "In a niche typically dominated by female consumers, we decided to develop a new Greek yogurt specifically suited to address the unique health and nutrition needs of the most neglected consumers in the category: men." Yogurt producer Danone quickly followed suit with its Danone for Men yogurt product line, launched in Bulgaria in August 2013.

≡ SEX AND YOGURT ≡

According to a research review published in the journal *PLOS ONE* in 2014, male mice fed a yogurt diet developed larger testicles, higher testosterone levels, and higher sperm concentrations. The authors hypothesized that the fertility benefits in the mice could be due to yogurt's probiotic bacteria.

≡ JUST FOR HER ≡

Activia, the first yogurt targeted specifically to women, was launched in France by the multinational food company Danone in 1987. Containing a proprietary strain of *Bifidobacterium*, the yogurt was designed to improve the digestive health of women. Danone later came under fire about its health claims about Activia, which have been the subject of several lawsuit and class action claims.

BUZZ BARS (*noun*): Bipolar coffeehouses that serve alcohol in addition to coffee.

═ ORIGINS ═

One of the earliest references to "buzz bars" appeared in a 2012 trend article in the *Indianapolis Star* on the emergence of a series of cafés in central Indiana—including Hearthstone Coffee House and Pub—serving wine, beer, and spirits along with the usual coffee.

═ LATTES AND LIBATIONS ═

In 2010, coffee chain Starbucks launched its "Starbucks Evenings" program in Seattle, serving beer and wine along with its usual coffee menu, as well as small plates and desserts. It later rolled out the program in select locations in Los Angeles, Portland, Chicago, and Atlanta. "We will still be your neighborhood gathering place with an inviting atmosphere for people of all ages," declared the Starbucks website. "After 4 p.m., you'll experience a more mellow, less hurried atmosphere perfect for winding down and having casual conversations."

═ PAIRINGS ═

For devotees of coffee and beer, combining the two drinks can be a marriage made in heaven.

Sidle up to the counter at Tryst, a buzz bar in Washington, DC, and order the Dufrain, and you'll receive a pint of Guinness with an espresso shot.

A number of craft breweries have introduced beers brewed with coffee, such as Goose Island Beer Company's Bourbon County Brand Coffee Stout, Evil Twin Brewing's Imperial Biscotti Break, and Cigar City Brewing's Cubano-Style Espresso Brown Ale.

In 2014, Starbucks began testing the Dark Barrel Latte, a nonalcoholic coffee drink incorporating "toasty stout flavors" and "inspired by the rise of craft beers." Immediate reviews on Twitter were mixed, ranging from "like drinking a Guinness in the early morning... So yuck" to "like a beer but with espresso #notbad" and "just like beer & I might be in love."

CAKE SPLOSH•ING

(*noun*): The act of sitting on a cake for the purpose of art, a prank, or sexual gratification.

≡ THE ART OF THE SPLOSH ≡

As part of her *Performing Audience* exhibit held at New York's Trestle Gallery in 2014, artist Martha Burgess held a "cake sit," at which participants were invited to bring their own cakes and smash them with their backsides. "I'm drawn to the object that is produced as a result of the process, and I feel that this result may be more important than the accident itself," Burgess told writer Charlotte Druckman, who reported on the event for the *Paris Review*.

≡ SPORTS SPLOSH ≡

Sparky Lyle, relief pitcher for the 1970s New York Yankees, was famous for his locker room prank of getting naked and sitting on his teammates' birthday cakes. In his 1979 book about the Yankees, *The Bronx Zoo*, he expounded on his sploshing technique: "I strive for leaving a perfect ass print on the cake after I sit on it. If the icing goes right up in that little point where your ass cracks, then you've done it right. And it takes practice to do that."

≡ WET AND MESSY ≡

Sploshing is a catch-all term for the subgenre of sexual fetishism known as "wet and messy" fetishes. People with these predilections are typically drawn to the tactile sensations of wet, messy substances against their skins. In addition to frosted cakes, sploshing may include cream pies, chocolate sauce, whipped cream, ketchup, ice cream, or other foodstuffs.

CARN·ISM (*noun*): An ideology or system of beliefs that supports the choice to consume meat.

....

≡ ORIGINS ≡

Carnism was coined by Melanie Joy, PhD, a social psychologist and author of *Why We Love Dogs, Eat Pigs, and Wear Cows*. "Carnism is the invisible belief system, or ideology, that conditions us to eat certain animals," argues Joy. "It is the opposite of veganism. We tend to label only those ideologies that fall outside the norm, as though the dominant culture doesn't have a belief system. For instance, we tend to assume that only vegans and vegetarians bring their beliefs to the dinner table—but most of us don't eat pigs but not dogs because we don't have a belief system when it comes to eating animals. When eating animals is not a necessity for survival—which is the case in much of the world today—then it is a choice. And choices always stem from beliefs."

≡ MEAT PTSD ≡

The Carnism Awareness and Action Network claims that individuals working in the meat processing industry who have witnessed violence against animals can suffer from "carnism-induced trauma," a form of post-traumatic stress disorder: "Symptoms include intrusive thoughts or images, flashbacks, hyperarousal (one's nervous system being on 'high alert'), numbing or constriction (feeling emotionally 'flat,' disconnected from one's feelings and from others), loss of faith in humanity and/or in any meaning or order in the universe, survivor guilt (feeling guilty for not being a direct victim), and depression."

≡ NEOCARNISM ≡

Animal welfare advocates have coined the term *neocarnism* to critique the ideology behind the production of humanely raised meat. The website Humanemyth.org defines neocarnism thusly: "A belief system characteristic of former animal rights advocates who collaborate with various segments of the animal-using industry and participate in development, certification, endorsement, or promotion of alternative 'humane' animal products, sometimes called 'happy meat.'"

CAR•ROT•MOB (*noun*):

A "reverse boycott" where a group of people gather to financially support an environmentally friendly store by purchasing its goods.

≡ ORIGINS ≡

The first official carrotmob is believed to have taken place in 2008 at San Francisco's K & D Market, where some three hundred shoppers assembled at a prearranged time to spend $9,276.50 in just a couple of hours. Brent Schulkin, the organizer of the event (and founder of Carrotmob.org), previously met with shops in the neighborhood to "bid" on his flash mob of shoppers in exchange for a pledge to increase energy efficiency. K & D bid highest by pledging that 22 percent of the day's sales would be used to improve its lighting system and hazardous waste disposal.

≡ EVOLUTION ≡

Carrotmobs have their roots in flash mobs, which originated in 2003 with groups of people gathering together—seemingly spontaneously—for a brief time for the purpose of satire, artistic expression, or a massive pillow fight.

≡ WEB-BASED ≡

Carrotmobs have become a worldwide movement, ranging from reverse boycotts at an Australian crepe stand offering biodegradable packaging to a Canadian coffee shop promising efficiency upgrades. While Carrotmob.org, a clearinghouse for information on ongoing and upcoming events is no longer active, a French version, Carrotmob.fr, has emerged, and individuals interested in staging and participating in carrotmobs can find information on current events and activities around the globe via social media using the hashtag #carrotmob.

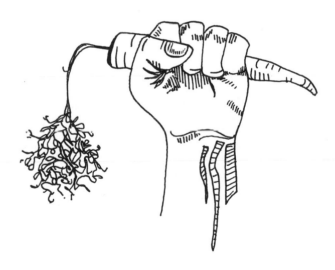

CAT CA•FÉ (*noun*): A themed café where cats may be viewed or played with.

≡ ORIGINS ≡

The first cat café, the Cat Flower Garden, opened in Taiwan in 1998 and quickly emerged as a tourist attraction for Japanese visitors. Feline café culture eventually migrated to Japan in 2005 with the opening of Cat's Store, Tokyo's first cat café. There are now more than thirty-nine cat cafés in Tokyo, and the phenomenon has gone global, with cat-friendly coffee shops popping up across Asia, Europe, and the Americas. The first cat café to open in the United States, the Cat Town Café in Oakland, California, launched in 2014.

≡ HEAVY PETTING ≡

Cat cafés provide cat lovers with a place to relax for a sip of coffee or tea and feline companionship. Many seek to raise awareness about pet welfare issues, host cats from animal shelters, and offer opportunities for adoption. Cat cafés frequently require reservations so that the cats do not receive excessive attention.

≡ CREATURE COMFORT ≡

Cat cafés have spawned a number of variations on the theme. Rabbit cafés and goat cafés have cropped up in Tokyo, as well as the Moomin House Café, a so-called "anti-loneliness" café where solo customers can sit down with Moomins, enormous plush stuffed animals based on the hippo-like Finnish children's book characters. For dog lovers, the Bau House in Seoul, South Korea, offers a canine alternative where patrons can grab a cup of coffee and buy treats for dogs who roam freely through the space.

CHER·PUM·PLE (*noun*): The turducken of desserts. A three-layer cake with pies baked into each layer—a cherry pie baked inside a white cake, a pumpkin pie baked inside a yellow cake, and an apple pie baked inside a spice cake. The whole thing is coated with cream-cheese frosting.

≡ ORIGINS ≡

Los Angeles resident and home baker Charles Phoenix invented the cherpumple in 2009. Making the dessert can take up to three days because each layer must cool before being baked into another. "It both intrigues and horrifies people," Phoenix told the *Wall Street Journal* in 2010. "It puts the kitsch in kitchen."

≡ PUMPECAPPLE PIECAKE ≡

In 2011, Houston's Three Brothers Bakery created the "pumpecapple piecake," a three-layer frosted cake comprised of a pumpkin pie baked into a pumpkin spice cake, a pecan pie baked into a chocolate cake, and an apple pie baked into an apple spice cake.

≡ BAKE IT IN A CAKE ≡

Megan Seling created Bakeitinacake.com, a blog devoted to things baked in other things, in 2010 and published a cookbook, *Bake it in a Cupcake*, in 2012. She has baked everything from baklava to candy bars and pancakes into cupcakes.

☰ ENGASTRATION ☰

The cherpumple is a sweet variation on engastration, the cooking of an animal inside another animal. While the turducken, a twentieth-century creation consisting of a chicken stuffed inside a duck stuffed inside a turkey, may be the most popular example of the technique, Alexandre Balthazar Laurent Grimod de la Reynière published an infamous recipe in 1807 for *rôti sans pareil* ("roast without equal") consisting of seventeen different birds rammed inside one another and roasted.

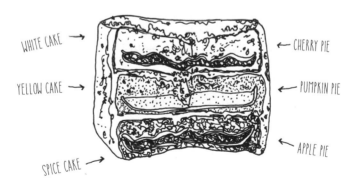

WHITE CAKE →
YELLOW CAKE →
SPICE CAKE →
← CHERRY PIE
← PUMPKIN PIE
← APPLE PIE

CLUB AP•PLE (*noun*):

A variety of apple developed through interbreeding and controlled through patents and trademarks so that it may only be produced and sold by an exclusive group of farmers.

≡ ORIGINS ≡

The Honeycrisp, a hybrid of Macoun and Honeygold apples renowned for its crisp texture and sweet flavor, is considered the first club apple. Patented by the University of Minnesota in 1998, Honeycrisp growers were required to pay the university a licensing fee of about a dollar per tree in order to grow them. Tight control is said to improve quality and keep supply consistent, while keeping apple prices high.

≡ TRADEMARKS ≡

Newer varieties of club apple are tightly controlled and managed. The SweeTango apple, for example, is not only covered with a patent but also a trademark. The select group of growers that produce the apples must pay royalties to the University of Minnesota, which developed the SweeTango.

≡ CLUB KIDS ≡

Some members of the club:

+ Ambrosia
+ Autumn Glory
+ Cosmic Crisp
+ EverCrisp
+ Frostbite
+ Honeycrisp
+ Jazz
+ KIKU
+ Lady Alice
+ RubyFrost
+ SnapDragon
+ SnowSweet
+ SweeTango
+ Zestar!

COF•FEE NAME (*noun*):

An alias given when ordering a coffee drink when one's real name is too difficult for the barista to pronounce and/or transcribe on a coffee cup.

═ ORIGINS ═

A 2006 entry on the website Urbandictionary.com credits Marina Maggiore with this term for easing the ordering process when dealing with a spelling-challenged barista: "This morning I went to Starbucks for my morning latte. I told the clerk that my name is Antoinette, which he could not spell. So I used my coffee name: Toni. Much easier to pronounce."

═ STARBUCKS SPELLING ═

The website Starbucksspelling.tumblr.com collects photos of coffee cups emblazoned with the misspelled names that prompt so many customers to invent a coffee name. Here are a few:

REAL NAME	MISSPELLED NAME
Corinne	Kharen
Allison	Allerson
Hillary	Hellery
Isaac	Icic
Margaux	Marabcdefgh
Todd	Tobb
Alicia	Ilisia

REAL NAME	MISSPELLED NAME
Justin	Jasitan
Cherie	Shirry
Bonnie	Pony

"I was in line at Starbucks, and they asked for my name. And spelling 'Shefali' just took forever. And I think at one point, somebody in the line—in the back of the line—was saying, hurry up—like, let's go. And that's when it dawned on me. I'm like, 'You know what? Forget this. I'm just going to use a fake name. I can't take this anymore.' So the next time I ordered coffee, the first thing that came to mind was Sheila."

—SHEFALI KULKARNI (A.K.A. "SHEILA"), STARBUCKS CUSTOMER

Josh Friedland

COF•FEE NAP (*noun*): A short nap preceded by drinking a cup of coffee in order to minimize drowsiness after waking. Also known as "caffeine napping."

HOW TO TAKE A COFFEE NAP

According to Joseph Stromberg, who wrote about the benefits of coffee naps for Vox.com in 2014:

1. Pour yourself a cup of coffee (while tea and soda may be caffeinated, they have much less caffeine than coffee).
2. Drink the coffee quickly to give yourself a window of time to sleep as it is digested. Iced coffee or espresso is recommended if downing a cup of hot coffee is too difficult.
3. Immediately try to nap.
4. Set an alarm to wake up within twenty minutes, before entering deeper stages of sleep.

≡ SLEEP SCIENCE ≡

Studies at the Sleep Research Laboratory at Loughborough University in Leicestershire, UK, found that participants who took a coffee nap committed fewer errors on a driving simulator than others who were given only a nap or coffee. Moreover, a study at Hiroshima University in Japan found that people were less tired and performed better on memory tests after a coffee nap as compared to a traditional nap.

≡ HOW IT WORKS ≡

Consumption of caffeine has the effect of blocking receptors in the brain for adenosine, a nucleoside that ordinarily accumulates while you're awake and makes you feel tired. After a cup of coffee, the sleepiness that would normally be caused by adenosine is dissipated and the stimulating effect of caffeine (which usually kicks in about thirty minutes after drinking coffee) is enhanced. According to David Dinges, PhD, a professor in the department of psychiatry at the University of Pennsylvania, "if you can fall asleep in your nap before caffeine does that, when it's time to wake up, you're getting the benefits of the caffeine perfectly timed with the nap sleep benefit."

COOK•I•VORES (*noun*):
The classification of humans as a species that evolved to cook and eat cooked food.

....

≡ ORIGINS ≡

The term was coined by Richard Wrangham, a professor of biological anthropology at Harvard University and author of *Catching Fire: How Cooking Made Us Human*, who argues that humans evolved to eat cooked foods. According to Wrangham, the innovation of cooking had the effect of making food softer and easier to digest, paving the way for the evolution of *Homo erectus*, who could consume the high energy diet needed to support a bigger brain without chewing raw food all day. He and his colleagues determined that if *Homo erectus* did not eat cooked food, he would have needed to eat a massive amount of raw food—roughly twelve pounds of raw plant food a day or six pounds of raw plants plus raw meat—to get enough calories to survive.

≡ FIRE STARTERS ≡

The cookivore theory depends upon a chronology of human history in which early hominids mastered fire (and the ability to cook food) as long as 1.6 to 1.9 million years ago. This time frame is disputed by other scientists. The earliest archeological evidence of fire—charred bone and primitive stone tools discovered in a cave in South Africa in 2012—dates back roughly one million years.

≡ PRIMITIVE PROTECTION RACKET ≡

Wrangham also credits cooking with shaping social relations between males and females. By providing quicker calories than raw food, males had more time to focus on hunting while females focused on gathering and cooking. Moreover, he argues that a sort of "primitive protection racket" emerged whereby primitive husbands "used their bonds with other men in the community to protect their wives from being robbed (of food they gathered), and women returned the favor by preparing their husbands' meals." Ultimately, says Wrangham, "Cooking created and perpetuated a novel system of male cultural superiority."

COW•POOL•ING (*noun*):

The practice of individuals banding together as a group to purchase a side of beef or whole cow and share the meat.

≡ ORIGINS ≡

The earliest media references to cowpooling date to 2008, including a *New York Times* article on the growth of businesses catering to urban locavores. "A share in a cow raised in a nearby field can be brought to you, ready for the freezer—a phenomenon dubbed cow pooling," wrote *New York Times* reporter Kim Severson. "There is pork pooling as well."

≡ BY THE NUMBERS ≡

According to online meat purveyor Askthemeatman.com, a typical steer weighing 1,150 lbs. will produce a 715-pound carcass yielding approximately 569 lbs. of meat and 146 lbs. of fat, bone, and loss:

+ 209.5 lbs. chuck
+ 155.8 lbs. round
+ 134.6 lbs. thin cuts (e.g., flank steak, skirt steak, and brisket)
+ 115.7 lbs. short loin
+ 66.6 lbs. rib meat
+ 27 lbs. offal

≡ COST SAVINGS ≡

Among the benefits of cowpooling are savings on the price of meat over supermarkets and butchers. A 2009 article published by the Mother Nature Network estimated that strip steak purchased via cowpooling costs between three dollars and five dollars per pound compared to sixteen dollars per pound at a retail market.

"As a person of rural origin who has lived much of my life in rural places...I can't tell you how joyful it makes me to hear that it's trendy for people in Manhattan to own a part of a cow."

—BARBARA KINGSOLVER, AUTHOR

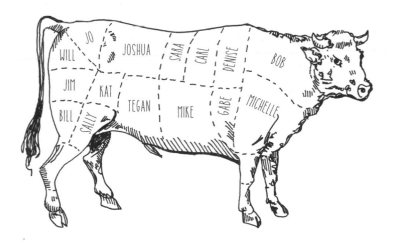

CRIN•CHY (*adjective*): An industry term for snack food products with a texture that falls somewhere between crisp and crunchy.

≡ ORIGINS ≡

National Starch (now Ingredion), an ingredient provider to food and beverage companies and other industries, coined the term in 2008 to describe the unique texture of foods that straddle the textures of crispy and crunchy. Ingredion works with food manufacturers to achieve the perfect level of crinchiness in their snack products by introducing specialty starch texturizers that optimize moisture content throughout the manufacturing process.

≡ TEXICON ≡

The term *crinchy* is part of Ingredion's TEXICON food texture language, which the firm designed as "a way to translate the consumer texture experience into measurable scientific terms." In addition to *crinchy*, TEXICON includes such novel terms as *flumpy*, which was coined to "pinpoint a particular characteristic of mayonnaise as it is spooned from the jar."

☰ THE ELEMENTS OF CRINCH ☰

According to Ingredion, these are the eight key textural attributes of crinchy foods:

+ Hardness
+ Fracturability
+ Denseness
+ Volume
+ Pitch
+ Cracks per bite
+ Duration of sound
+ Dissolvability

"If you think about the consumer vernacular for crackers and snacks it is crispy or crunch and nothing else. We have discovered 18 factors that go into crispy and crunchy. We can then present to a food formulator actionable and measurable steps they can take to get the texture that consumers would like."

—MARC GREEN, INGREDION SPOKESMAN

CRO·NUT (*noun*): A croissant-doughnut hybrid pastry.

≡ ORIGINS ≡

Chef Dominique Ansel created the Cronut in 2013 at his Dominique Ansel Bakery in New York City. It is a ring-shaped pastry made of "laminated dough" that resembles a croissant, deep fried in grape seed oil, rolled in sugar, filled with cream, and topped with a glaze. Ansel trademarked the Cronut in 2014.

≡ OF DOSANTS AND DOUGHSSANTS ≡

Chef Alina Eisenhauer says that she has been serving a nearly identical mash-up, the "dosant," at her Sweet Kitchen & Bar in Worcester, Massachusetts, since 2008. Moreover, Roy Auddino says his Auddino's Bakery & Cafe in Ohio has been making and selling a croissant-doughnut hybrid under the name "doughssant" since 1991.

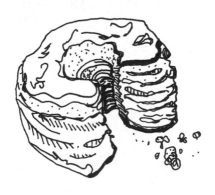

≡ MORE MASH-UPS ≡

The Cronut rode a wave of food mash-ups combining unlikely ingredients into popular food marriages:

Baco: A taco with a shell made of bacon.

Ramen burger: A hamburger patty between two fried noodle "buns."

Phorrito: A burrito filled with noodles, thin sliced beef, and other pho ingredients (hold the soup).

Foieffle: A foie gras–stuffed waffle.

Pizzabon: A savory cinnamon bun filled with tomato sauce and cheese.

Sushirito: Rice and raw fish wrapped in a large nori "tortilla."

Cragel: Croissant in the shape of a bagel.

Luther burger: A burger on a doughnut bun.

Pretzel croissant: A croissant seasoned with salt and sesame seeds.

≡ PASTRY SCALPING ≡

Baked daily in limited batches of two hundred, the Cronut drew huge lines of customers arriving at dawn in hope of getting a taste of the popular pastry. A Cronut black market soon cropped up, offering the opportunity to nab a Cronut, which retails for five dollars, for the princely sum of one hundred dollars.

CROP MOB (*noun*): An event where volunteers come together at a small farm to donate their time to make agricultural enhancements.

....

≡ ORIGINS ≡

According to the website Cropmob.org, the first crop mob took place in October 2008 when a group of nineteen farmers, farm apprentices, and members of the larger agricultural community joined together at Piedmont Biofarm in Pittsboro, North Carolina, to harvest sweet potatoes. Since that event, more than fifty crop mob groups have emerged around the United States. The events typically draw twenty-something millennials looking for the opportunity to take part in a community-based activity, get some sun, and dip their toes into farming, if for only a day.

≡ MODERN BARN RAISING ≡

Crop mobs are a reinvention of a very old idea, barn raising, with a contemporary twist: through crop mobbing websites and social media, like-minded agricultural enthusiasts find each other online and descend upon a farm for a day of real-world volunteering. A 2010 *New York Times Magazine* article on the crop mob trend reported that volunteers had contributed more than two thousand hours of agricultural work at small, sustainable farms, "doing tasks like mulching, building greenhouses, and pulling rocks out of fields."

"It's just an opportunity for city mice to get out to a farm and get their hands dirty… We focus on small, sustainable organic farms. We want to help farmers, and we ask for jobs that don't require training and aren't dangerous. It's idiot work, and we're the idiots."

—BARTH ANDERSON, CROP MOBBER

= MOB FARMS =

Crop mobs should not be mistaken for "mob farms," a structure in the video game *Minecraft* built for spawning characters known as mobs.

CROP SWAP (*noun*): A market where individuals trade in surplus fruits and vegetables from their urban farms. Events may take the form of a barter exchange or resemble a potluck.

≡ ORIGINS ≡

The *New York Times* traced the origins of the crop swap back to colonial era food exchanges between pilgrims and American Indians, but according to the *San Francisco Chronicle*, the modern version was an outgrowth of the Transition movement, a grassroots drive for sustainability that launched in England in 2005. Crop swaps eventually took hold in California, beginning with the Oak Park neighborhood of Sacramento in 2008 and later in Berkeley in 2011. The global reach of crop swaps has continued apace, with reports of the produce exchanges popping up in Taranaki, New Zealand, in 2013.

≡ SWAP NETWORKING ≡

In 2011, Emily Han, a writer and recipe developer in Los Angeles, cofounded Foodswapnetwork.com as an online resource for people to find local swaps or set up new ones.

≡ SEED SWAPS ≡

A seed swap is an event where gardeners meet to exchange seeds, typically to trade in old heirloom varieties. In the

United States, the last Saturday in January is celebrated as "National Seed Swap Day."

≡ HOMONYM ≡

Communitarian crop swaps among like-minded locavores should not be confused with the U.S. military's "crop swap" strategy of luring poppy farmers in Afghanistan to replace their crops with sustainable alternatives.

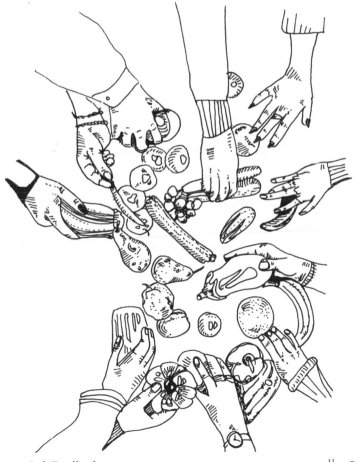

DEM•I•TAR•I•AN

(*adjective*): Of or relating to a diet limiting meat consumption to half the standard portion eaten at regular meals.

≡ ORIGINS ≡

Professor Mark Sutton is credited with coining the concept of a demitarian diet, whereby one reduces meat consumption by half in order to stem environmental damage associated with meat production. Demitarianism was advocated by the UN Environment Programme in a study published in 2013 and coauthored by Sutton.

≡ BARSAC DECLARATION ≡

The term appeared in 2009 in the Barsac Declaration, developed in Barsac, France, at the combined workshop of Nitrogen in Europe and Biodiversity in European Grasslands: Impacts of Nitrogen: "We declare our commitment to: a. Encourage the availability of reduced portion sizes of meat and animal products, compared with current standards in developed countries, for the preparation of healthy meals, b. Implement this commitment through promotion of the 'demitarian' option, which we define as a meal containing half the amount of meat or fish compared with the normal local alternative, combined with a correspondingly larger amount of other food products..."

≡ ENVIRONMENTAL IMPACT ≡

A 2014 report by the UN Economic Commission for Europe, *Nitrogen on the Table*, found that if a demitarian diet was adopted throughout Europe and meat and dairy intake was cut by 50 percent, it would reduce greenhouse gas emissions by 25 to 40 percent and lower soybean imports (mostly used to feed livestock) by 75 percent.

DRUNK•OREX•IA (*noun*):

The practice of restricting food intake (by skipping meals or bingeing and purging) to allow for increased calorie consumption through drinking alcohol while maintaining weight.

≡ ORIGINS ≡

The earliest references to the phenomenon of drunkorexia date to 2007, with more widespread attention by the *New York Times* and other mainstream media outlets in 2008, calling attention to alcohol abuse combined with disordered eating.

≡ SCIENCE ≡

While *drunkorexia* may not be a strict medical term, researchers have explored the link between eating disorders and binge drinking, focusing mainly on female college students, a population where it appears to be most prevalent. According to a 2010 study by East Carolina University and Oklahoma State University researchers published in the *Journal of Alcohol and Drug Education*, of 692 freshmen at a southeastern university, 14.2 percent of first-year students sampled restricted their caloric intake on days they knew alcohol consumption would occur. Of these, 70 percent were female and 29 percent were male.

A first of its kind study in Australia published by Alissa Knight and Susan Simpson in the *Journal of Eating Disorders* in 2013 found that of 139 healthy female college students studied, 79.1 percent reported engaging in drunkorexia behavior.

"I had my 'drinking day' menu down to a fine art. A banana and handful of cereal with skimmed milk for breakfast, a salad for lunch, and for dinner a 75 g baked potato, a poached egg, and a huge heap of steamed leeks. Total calories: 560. The estimated average daily requirement for women is 1,940 calories, so that left me with 1,380 calories to play with and I chose to spend them on alcohol. That's more than two bottles of wine."

—JASMINE GARDNER, RECOVERING DRUNKOREXIC

DUCK•EASY (*noun*):

A speakeasy or underground event for serving foie gras in locales where the fattened liver delicacy has been banned.

≡ ORIGINS ≡

The first reports of the existence of duckeasies appeared in Chicago in 2007 following the city's ban on the sale of foie gras. Duckeasies emerged in San Francisco in 2012 after California's statewide prohibition on the production and sale of foie gras came into effect.

≡ CONTROVERSY ≡

There is a long-standing debate over whether gavage, the force-feeding method by which the liver of a duck or goose is fattened to produce foie gras, is humane. In response to the controversy, the Chicago City Council banned the sale of foie gras in 2006, but the prohibition was repealed in 2008. California's statewide ban on production and sale of foie gras was enacted in 2006 but overturned in 2015 by a federal district judge. Globally, production of foie gras is banned in Israel, Germany, and England; its importation is prohibited in India.

═ DUCKEASY DEVOTEE ═

After attending a San Francisco duckeasy in 2012, blogger Johnny Gnall hailed the gastronomic pleasures of prohibition: "So raise your torchons, your lobes, your burgers dripping goose fat, and your chocolate-covered foie gras bonbons (yes, they exist). And toast the ban on foie…because it's never been so good!"

═ FOIEKAGE FEE ═

Some California restaurants used a loophole in the law to charge diners a "foiekage fee" (akin to a corkage fee for wine) to prepare liver purchased in other states.

EGO·TAR·I·AN CUI·SINE (*noun*): A term used to describe food—usually found on tasting menus—created by male chefs to indulge their own egos in spite of their customers.

....

≡ ORIGINS ≡

GQ magazine restaurant critic Alan Richman coined the phrase in a 2014 column decrying the rise of (mostly) male chefs whose self-indulgent tendencies in the kitchen get the best of them: "This style of dining is currently nameless. What makes the food different is that every chef is seeking to express himself in an incomparable and triumphant manner. I call it Egotarian Cuisine… The chefs behind it, many of them acclaimed, test culinary boundaries, push themselves to the edge of the cliff, and sometimes drop off. You'll come upon this food if you're heading for a restaurant that serves small-plate dishes that express the inspirations of the chef, and if what appears before you are compilations of ingredients never previously compiled."

≡ ERGO, EGO ≡

In his article, Richman cataloged nine signposts of egotarian cuisine. Among them:

+ "You're eating from earthenware bowls crafted by women living in upstate woodlands."

- "The herb in your soup is found only in botany textbooks."
- "The chef explains that his cooking has 'a story to tell,' and it's a romantic novel of self-love."

"I've come to hate tasting menus. Yes, I know, that we should all have these problems. Ooh my diamond slippers are pinching and all that. But really! Hell is being pelted with itsy-bitsy food doodles, the culinary equivalent of a Fisher-Price activity centre for grown-ups: sniff that, suck on this, lick the other, shiny, shiny, shiny. If something you actually like turns up, there's never enough of it. The damn thing has gone before you've registered it was there. And you have to be reverent and sombre and serious because it's all about the bloody chef locating the wellspring of their creativity. Well, I know what I'd like to do with their wellspring."

—JAY RAYNER, RESTAURANT CRITIC

FARM GALS (*noun*): Urban (but rural-curious) young Japanese women with an interest in fashion and farming.

....

≡ ORIGINS ≡

The term *farm gals*—*Nogyaru*, in Japanese—is a combination of the words *nogyo* ("agriculture") and *gyaru* ("gals"). A 2010 article titled "Fashionista Farm Gals of Tokyo," appearing on the United Nations University online magazine *Our World 2.0*, reported on the emergence of the phenomenon: "In rice fields almost 700 kilometres away from the Japanese capital Tokyo, you can find 20-something city girls working hard in a swirl of dust. You can't miss them because their fashion inevitably stands out in a paddy—colourful clothes and high heeled boots, over-dyed blonde hair, lush eye lashes, and long polished nails. Reflexively, you may cast a hasty second glance, because they are so unexpected. Are they really farmers, you may ask? The answer is YES."

≡ POPGRICULTURE ≡

In 2009, the *Japan Times* reported that Shiho Fujita, then a twenty-four-year-old pop singer (stage name "sifow"), was growing rice on a farm in the Akita Prefecture sold under the brand Shibuya Rice, denoting Tokyo's fashion and shopping district. She is also the author of a book on "gal farming" and the designer of farming couture: stretch denim overalls with pockets for mobile phones. "Young people, including me in the past, don't have a clear picture about agriculture in general and the food problems we face," Fujita told *Our World 2.0.* "That's what I want to change."

═ HELLO GRITTY ═

In 2014, Sanrio and farmer Raymond Cheng partnered to open the Hello Kitty Go Green Organic Farm in Hong Kong, the world's first Hello Kitty–themed farm. Children can enroll in the Hello Kitty Little Farmer Program, where they get to take care of their own five-square-foot plot.

FAST-FOOD ZON•ING

(*noun*): The use of local zoning regulations by cities to promote healthier food options by restricting the number of fast-food outlets in neighborhoods.

≡ ORIGINS ≡

In 2008, the Los Angeles City Council passed a one-year moratorium on the opening of new fast-food restaurants in South Los Angeles, a large section of Los Angeles with higher rates of poverty and obesity than other neighborhoods. The ban was made permanent in 2010.

"There are people who are accused of being the food police, of trying to control what goes into people's mouths," Bernard Parks, a city councilman who represents parts of South Los Angeles, told the *New York Times* in 2011. "But we just don't think that we need to give fast food more rights around here. We don't think our community needs to have 10 or 15 or 18 ways to eat a hamburger."

≡ HISTORY ≡

Many communities have used zoning laws to prohibit fast-food restaurants, dating back to 1981 in Concord, Massachusetts, and 1987 in San Francisco's Geary Boulevard Fast-Food Subdistrict. Unlike the landmark South Los Angeles ban, these measures were not established as part of a health policy but to preserve local flavor and protect small businesses from the intrusion of chains.

═ SCIENCE ═

On the heels of the fast-food restrictions, a 2009 study by the RAND Corporation questioned the empirical evidence for the ban, finding that the density of fast-food chain restaurants per capita was actually higher in other parts of Los Angeles than in South LA. It also suggested that enacting other regulations, such as menu calorie labeling, would have a stronger impact on reducing obesity.

A subsequent study by RAND published in 2015 declared that fast-food zoning had "failed to reduce fast-food consumption or reduce obesity rates in the targeted neighborhoods." Moreover, the researchers found that "since the fast-food restrictions were passed in 2008, overweight and obesity rates in South Los Angeles and other neighborhoods targeted by the law have increased faster than in other parts of the city or other parts of the county."

FAT WASH•ING (*noun*):

A technique for flavoring spirits with ingredients that have a high fat content (e.g., bacon) whereby the fat is rendered, mixed with the alcohol, and then removed after a period of freezing.

≡ ORIGINS ≡

A 2007 article by Nick Fauchald in *Food & Wine* magazine explained how bartender Eben Freeman (of the now-shuttered Tailor restaurant) used fat washing to flavor spirits: "Among the bag of tricks Freeman packed for Tailor is a process called 'fat washing,' an ingenious way to flavor spirits that he borrowed from one of [chef Sam] Mason's desserts. By mixing a melted fat with alcohol, chilling the mixture until the fat resolidifies, then skimming it off, Freeman can infuse a spirit without leaving any greasiness behind."

Freeman credits fat washing to Mason, who took inspiration from the techniques of perfumers.

≡ BENTON'S OLD FASHIONED ≡

The Benton's Old Fashioned may well be one of the most famous cocktails using fat-washed spirits. Created by Don Lee in 2011 at New York's PDT bar, the libation combines bourbon washed with bacon from Benton's in Tennessee, maple syrup, and bitters served on the rocks with an orange twist.

≡ VEGAN FAT WASHING? ≡

Writing in *Details* magazine in 2014, Camper English reported that bartenders were moving beyond fat washing with animal fats to incorporate plant-based fats from coconuts, olive oil, cocoa, and nuts. "Naren Young at Bacchanal in Manhattan makes the house Mai Tai with almond-fat washed rum, orange curacao, chili liqueur, lime, yuzu, and smoked orgeat," wrote English. "I'm nuts for it."

≡ HISTORY ≡

While the technique of fat washing might be novel, carnivorous cocktails are nothing new. In the 1940s, Giuseppe Cipriani invented the Bull Shot at Harry's Bar in Venice by blending beef consommé with vodka, Worcestershire, and Tabasco sauce served on ice.

FELF•IE (*noun*): A photographic self-portrait of a farmer, typically taken with a smartphone and shared via social media.

= ORIGINS =

The felfie phenomenon took off in 2014 when the *Irish Farmers Journal* hosted a Facebook competition for best "Selfie on the Farm." P. J. Ryan of Newport, County Tipperary, won the competition with a felfie featuring his pipe-smoking visage and a number of Salers cattle in the background.

= SOCIAL MEDIA =

Felfies can be found on Twitter and Instagram with the hashtag #felfie. In addition, the website Felfies.com curates the very best felfies on the Internet, organized by nationality and livestock included.

= FELFIE POLITICS =

In 2014, farmers in British Columbia took to social media to post felfies in protest of a government proposal to divide the region's Agricultural Land Reserve into two zones. Seeing the move as a potential weakening of farm protections in the reserve, the farmers held up protest signs in their self-portraits to express their opposition.

"It's a bit of fun and puts a face to the farm and people like looking at photos of owners with their animals… It gives people a chance to see how things are on a farm and how things are looked after."

—AMANDA OWEN, FARMER AND FELFIE ENTHUSIAST

≡ HOMONYM ≡

The word has also been used by CenturyPly, an Indian manufacturer of veneers and plywood, to describe a self-portrait taken with your favorite furniture.

FLAT·BREAD FAC·TOR (*noun*): The popularity of flatbread products in developing countries as an indicator of increased urbanization and wealth.

≡ ORIGINS ≡

The term was coined by Alonso Martinez and Ronald Haddock of the consulting group Booz Allen Hamilton in their 2007 article "The Flatbread Factor" in *strategy+business*. They argued that when countries reach a certain point in their level of urbanization, sales of flatbreads rise as an inexpensive and convenient food for urban workers. Martinez and Haddock singled out the business strategy of GRUMA, a Mexican producer of tortillas, which has gone global targeting markets around the world with flatbreads: "Urbanization explains why Gruma's flatbread strategy is so powerful. Flatbread provides a quick and inexpensive meal; thus flatbread is one of the most popular premade food products that new city dwellers purchase."

≡ GLOBAL REACH ≡

GRUMA's global flatbread empire stretches from the Americas to Australia, with 101 plants and a presence in 113 countries worldwide. Its flatbread portfolio includes wraps, tortillas, naan, pizza dough, chapati, and piadina.

≡ HISTORY ≡

According to findings published in the *Proceedings of the National Academy of Sciences* journal in 2010, evidence of starch grains discovered on thirty-thousand-year-old grinding stones suggest that prehistoric humans may have eaten an early form of flatbread. "You make a kind of pita and cook it on the hot stone," Laura Longo, one of the researchers on the team, told Reuters.

"Urban families tend to have two incomes, with both adults working outside the home. This gives consumers more purchasing power, but also less time for food preparation and other household chores. Urban dwellers thus tend to buy more manufactured foods, particularly staples such as bread."

—ALONSO MARTINEZ AND RONALD HADDOCK,
VICE PRESIDENTS, BOOZ ALLEN HAMILTON

FLY·ING WINE·MAK·ERS (*noun*):

Itinerant winemakers who hire themselves out as consultants to wineries around the globe.

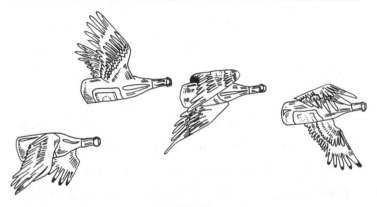

═ ORIGINS ═

The concept of the flying winemaker started in the 1990s with Australian winemakers traveling to wineries in the Northern Hemisphere to consult on new products during the Australian winter. Critics of flying winemakers argue that the involvement of a small group of consultants with so many different operations leads to the globalization of wine and homogenous products that exemplify the style of the winemaker rather than the region.

☰ HIGH-FLYER ☰

Michel Rolland, a Bordeaux-based oenologist (expert in wine science and production), is considered one of the most influential and successful flying winemakers, managing the quality of wine on up to two hundred wine estates worldwide. A 2006 article in *Wine Spectator* estimated that his consulting fees range from around $30,000 per year to as much as $150,000 per year.

☰ VINOTAINMENT ☰

The Flying Winemaker, an international wine and travel show, premiered in 2014 on Discovery Network's TLC Asia. The program is hosted by flying winemaker Eddie McDougall, a native of Hong Kong educated in Australia who is known for championing wines made in far-flung vineyards across Asia. His show has taken him from India to Mongolia, Vietnam, and Papua New Guinea to visit with regional winemakers and explore wine pairings with local foods.

FOOD BUB•BLE (*noun*):
The inflation of food production based on the unsustainable use of water and land.

....

≡ ORIGINS ≡

The concept of a food bubble is most closely associated with the work of environmental analyst Lester Brown, founder of the Earth Policy Institute. Brown first observed in the 2003 edition of his book *Plan B: Rescuing a Planet Under Stress and a Civilization in Trouble* that "many countries are in essence creating a 'food bubble economy'—one in which food production is artificially inflated by the unsustainable use of water." Brown further warned that climate change and the resulting decline in water tables could threaten water-intensive industrial agriculture, causing "the bursting of the food bubble."

≡ OVERPUMPING ≡

The World Bank reported in 2005 that 15 percent of India's food was being produced by overpumping groundwater. As a result, about 190 million Indians were being fed using water that could not be sustained.

"Tapping underground water resources helped expand world food production, but as the demand for grain continued climbing, so too did the amount of water pumped. Eventually the extraction of water began to exceed the recharge of aquifers from precipitation, and water tables began to fall. And then wells begin to go dry. In effect, overpumping creates a water-based food bubble, one that will burst when the aquifer is depleted and the rate of pumping is necessarily reduced to the rate of recharge."

—LESTER BROWN, ENVIRONMENTAL ANALYST

≡ HOMONYM ≡

Frederick Kaufman used the term *food bubble* to describe inflation in food prices in a 2010 article in *Harper's* titled "The Food Bubble: How Wall Street Starved Millions and Got Away With It."

FOOD•ING (*noun*): A movement to subvert the orthodoxy of traditional French gastronomy.

....

≡ ORIGINS ≡

A blending of the words *food* and *feeling*, *fooding* was coined in 1999 by French journalist and food critic Alexandre Cammas in the pages of *Nova Mag*. It has come to define a culinary movement whose goal is to upend conventional ideas about French food. Cammas told the *New Yorker* in 2010, "French cuisine was caught in a museum culture: the dictatorship of a fossilized idea of gastronomy. And this dictatorship has been enforced by tourism: you have tourists packing in to experience gastronomy in a kind of perpetual museum of edification. We wanted to be outside that, *sur le pont*, on the bridge, in front, defining everything that is new. We wanted to escape—foie gras, *volaille de bresse*, all the clichés."

≡ LE FOODING ≡

Since Cammas's coinage, "Le Fooding"—launched in 2000—has become the brand of an annual French restaurant guide and a series of culinary events that celebrate iconoclastic young French chefs and their upstart restaurants. Since 2008, the Paris-based organization has branched out internationally with Le Fooding events in New York, Los Angeles, Brussels, and Milan.

"The goal of the Fooding movement is to break down French snobbery, in the form of its hidebound hypersensitive discrimination, while the goal of the slow-food movement, though not put quite this way, is to build up hidebound hyper-discrimination. Fooding is a form of culinary Futurism: it wants the table to move as fast as modern life."

—ADAM GOPNIK, WRITER

See Also

bis·tron·o·my (page 12)

≡ DOGFOODING ≡

Unfortunately, "dogfooding" is not a neologism for a revolutionary pet food movement seeking to quash kibble. Rather, it's a tech industry term that means using the software you make in order to refine the product and eliminate glitches.

FOOD·I·OT (*noun*): A fervent gastronome whose outsized obsession with food infuriates others.

≡ ORIGINS ≡

Writer Joe Pompeo coined the term *foodiot* in a 2009 article in the *New York Observer* critiquing the proliferation of insufferable food fanboys (and girls) in New York City. He blamed the Internet and the rise of social media for the emergence of this new class of foodie with an unending appetite for public display of food fanaticism: "We see it in the meticulous record-keeping of eating habits on personal blogs. The ubiquitous Facebook updates and tweets about subscribers' most recent meals. (Surely you also have those five or so friends whose feeds are 90 percent food-consumption-related?) The requisite iPhone pic before a certain kind of diner—let's call him a foodiot—ravages his plate."

"Behind every foodie, there is probably a foodiot. We all have our own inner foodiots. You just have to stamp them down."

—MELISSA CLARK, FOOD WRITER

≡ INTERNATIONAL FOODIOCY ≡

A blogger named "Frankie" was so inspired by the *New York Observer* article that he embraced his inner foodiot and launched FoodiotKK.com in 2010. The food blog chronicles the local food scene in Kota Kinabalu, the capital of the state of Sabah in East Malaysia.

≡ SON OF FOODIOT ≡

The children of foodiots may very well be termed *koodies*, defined by "Supermarket Guru" Phil Lempert as "a kid keenly interested in food, especially eating, cooking, or watching reruns of Julia Child. A kid who has an ardent or refined interest in food; a mini-gourmet; usually trained by one or both parents to have an unusual, and sometimes fanatic, desire to eat unusual foods."

FOOD•OIR (*noun*):
Autobiographical writings that blend memoir with gastronomical commentary and recipes.

. . . .

≡ ORIGINS ≡

According to the vocabulary website Wordspy.com, the earliest reference to *foodoir* as a literary genre was in a 2002 article in the *Independent*: "A hybrid of memoir sensually larded with recipes, the foodoir belongs in the bedroom or on the beach, not the kitchen," wrote Caroline Stacey.

≡ HISTORY ≡

Writing for the *New York Times* in 2009, Christine Muhlke traced the evolution of culinary memoirs: "The foodoir was popularized by the likes of Frances Mayes and Ruth Reichl, who wrote eloquently of lazy Italian plumbers and revolutionary West Coast restaurants, punctuating their musings with recipes that brought the flavors of their stories onto the reader's plate—that is, if readers wanted to get their hardcover splattered. Bloggers took naturally to the format, weaving their personal lives into the cooking process as laid out onscreen. Book (and movie) deals followed."

≡ FIVE FOODOIRISTS ≡

Some notable foodoirists:

- Diana Abu-Jaber, author of *The Language of Baklava* (2006)

- Anthony Bourdain, author of *Kitchen Confidential: Adventures in the Culinary Underbelly* (2000)

- M. F. K. Fisher, foodoir pioneer and author of *The Gastronomical Me* (1943)

- Julie Powell, author of *Julie and Julia: 365 Days, 524 Recipes, 1 Tiny Apartment Kitchen* (2005), which became a feature film in 2009, and *Cleaving: A Story of Marriage, Meat, and Obsession* (2009)

- Ruth Reichl, the author of no less than three foodoirs: *Tender at the Bone: Growing Up at the Table* (1998), *Comfort Me with Apples: More Adventures at the Table* (2001), and *Garlic and Sapphires: The Secret Life of a Critic in Disguise* (2005)

FOOD RAC•ISM (*noun*):

An expression of racial prejudice that uses a stereotypical food item to make an insulting or disparaging remark or innuendo.

═ ORIGINS ═

In a 2009 column for CNN.com, Ruben Navarette Jr. discussed whether a controversial comment made by ESPN broadcaster Bob Griese about Colombian NASCAR driver Juan Pablo Montoya amounted to "food racism." When asked where Montoya was on a list of the top drivers in a NASCAR competition, Griese had said he was "out having a taco." On a food racism scale of one to ten, Navarette gave the slur a four.

═ CULINARY HEGEMONY ═

A 2013 commentary by Aaron Vansintjan for the *McGill Daily* posited that campaigns promoting so-called healthy foods might have a racist undertone: "Food racism happens when certain foods are excluded in favour of the dominant (white) culture's idea of good food."

═ RACIST FOODS ═

In a 2014 article, "Eating These Foods Might Make You Racist," for Vice.com, writer Dan Shapiro called out a series of foods, such as Australia's Coon Cheese, for using racial slurs and/or derogatory caricatures in their marketing. Of

Aunt Jemima syrup, Shapiro wrote, "above all else, the product's direct reference of plantation life, complete with not-so-hidden undertones of slavery, makes it the worst offender of food racism."

≡ DISCRIMINATING TASTES ≡

In 2012, a trade association of Austrian restaurateurs campaigned to ban offensive names for dishes such as *Zigeunerschnitzel* ("gypsy schnitzel") and *Mohr im Hemd* ("Moor-in-a-shirt," a chocolate and cream confection) from menus.

"When the Korean mailman says 'good morning,' I smile back and daydream of tender *bulgogi* wrapped in crisp lettuce. A steaming bowl of *bibimbap* topped with oozy egg yolk. Lacy kimchi pancakes.

"And when our kindly Trinidadian office security guard greets me, it's all I can do not to turn around and race right out for a bowl of callaloo.

"Does this make me some sort of food racist? Am I a foodist?"

—ANDREA SCOTTING, ADVERTISING COPYWRITER

FOOD SWAMP (*noun*):

A geographic area where the overabundance of junk food (for example, high-calorie snacks sold at convenience stores) inundates healthy food options.

≡ ORIGINS ≡

Authors Donald Rose, J. Nicholas Bodor, Chris M. Swalm, Janet C. Rice, Thomas A. Farley, and Paul L. Hutchinson coined the term in a 2009 paper titled "Deserts in New Orleans? Illustrations of Urban Food Access and Implications for Policy," as an alternative to "food desert," commonly defined as urban or rural areas without access to fresh, healthy, and affordable food.

"A more useful geographic metaphor," Rose et al. suggested, "would be 'food swamps,' areas in which large relative amounts of energy-dense snack foods inundate healthy food options."

≡ RESEARCH ≡

In 2009, the RAND Corporation published a study finding that the ban on the addition of fast-food outlets to the neighborhood of South Los Angeles (see fast-food zoning, page 70) was unlikely to reduce obesity rates so long as there was a large concentration of convenience and small grocery stores where "high-energy" snacks are plentiful. In an interview, Roland Strum, the author of the study, commented that the proliferation of convenience stores in poor urban areas had created food swamps: "It's less that people [live] in food deserts now, it's more that people live in food swamps… If we believe that the food environment is a major cause of obesity, then the big differences we see are in small convenience stores."

═ FOOD MIRAGE ═

Introducing healthy food options in neighborhoods may not always necessarily provide an immediate solution to the problems of food swamps or deserts. A 2014 study published in *Advances in Applied Sociology* investigated the arrival of New Seasons, an upscale supermarket, in the gentrifying Alberta neighborhood of Portland, Oregon, questioning whether it had improved access to healthy food: "Does the opening of a supermarket eliminate the food desert or does it instead create a food mirage, whereby minority and lower-class residents do not find it to be a viable option for their regular food shopping?"

FOOD VOICE (*noun*): A term for the ways in which an individual's food and drink patterns function as a mode of communication.

═ ORIGINS ═

Annie Hauck-Lawson, who coined *food voice*, wrote in 1992 that the term comprises "the dynamic, creative, symbolic, and highly individualized ways that food serves as a channel of communication." In particular, *food voice* captured the ways in which "food came forth as a powerful, highly charged, and personalized voice" of Polish American families she was studying as part of her dissertation research. She recalled that one member of the study, a Polish woman who had isolated herself in the kitchen after years of discord on an overcrowded farm, used her food voice to express her individuality through cooking: "It was so potent that at times it spoke without words."

═ CHEF VOICE ═

In a foreword to Hauck-Lawson's 2009 book *Gastropolis* (which she coedited with Jonathan Deutsch), New York City chef Michael Lomonaco declared his food voice: "I have long believed that New Yorkers can taste their way through most cuisines of the world without leaving the five boroughs. This global connection has influenced the food I cook at home as well as in the restaurant. I credit the food of New York for having informed and helped me find my own personal voice, the food voice that I rely on each day for my livelihood."

═ CULINARY *TESTIMONIOS* ═

Anthropologist Carole Counihan's ethnographic research in the town of Antonito, Colorado, published in 2007 in *Food and Culture: A Reader*, explored the food voice of Mexican American women through *testimonios*, "personal narratives that reveal individual subjectivity while calling attention to broad political and economic forces."

GAS·TRO-AN·O·MY

(*noun*): Individual anxiety fueled by open-ended food choices and the lack of clear criteria for nutritional decision making.

....

≡ ORIGINS ≡

Gastro-anomy (alternative spelling *gastro-anomie*) was coined by French social scientist Claude Fischler in an article published in 1980 in *Social Science Information*. The term captures the anxiety faced by individuals about food in modern society where they have become disconnected from the origins of food, family meals are on the decline, concerns about health and food safety abound, and the number of food choices has exploded. "One could say that the crisis of gastronomy leads to a state of gastro-anomy," wrote Fischler. "Modern individuals are left without clear sociocultural cues as to what their choice should be, as to when, how, and how much they should eat."

The word is a blending of *gastronomy* and *anomie*, the concept of "normlessness" popularized by sociologist Émile Durkheim to describe the condition of instability between the individual and society when social standards and values break down.

≡ ANTINOMIES OF TASTE ≡

In 2010, Tanja Schneider and Teresa Davis published an article in *Consumption Markets & Culture* exploring how the marketing of health-food products feeds into the condition of gastro-anomy. Scrutinizing issues of *Australia Women's Weekly*, a popular women's magazine in Australia, from 1951 to 2001, they concluded that the food industry's collaboration with scientists and nutritional experts on advertisements had created a "diet-making nexus" that created new norms for healthy food choices. They also identified a series of "antinomies of tastes"—messages about products that embody a tension in food choices (e.g., "indulgence" vs. "health") that consumers can neatly resolve by purchasing the advertised food (e.g., French fries cooked in "heart-healthy" sunflower oil that "you can eat to your heart's desire").

"The United States is a country where you can buy both soda with no calories *and* pizza with a crust stuffed with extra cheese. What's more, you can buy them *at the same place, at the same time.* That's about as anomic as it gets."

— SCOTT MCLEMEE, WRITER

GAS·TRO·SEX·U·AL

(*noun*): A person, typically male, who embraces cooking as a form of sexuality and deploys culinary aptitude to attract romantic partners.

≡ ORIGINS ≡

The term originated in a 2008 report by the Future Foundation titled *The Emergence of the Gastrosexual*. "Gastrosexuals can be male or female but the common denominator is their love of food." A spokesperson for PurAsia, a supermarket brand that funded the study, told the *Daily Mail*, "they cook for pleasure, praise, and potential seduction."

≡ MAKE (AND BAKE) OUT SESSION ≡

Peter Shafer, a winner of radio program the *Splendid Table*'s 2009 "Gastrosexual of the Month" contest, waxed about

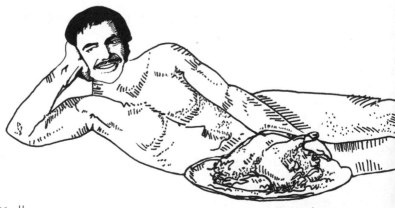

the romantic possibilities of making bread with a woman: "Your bread making allows you to get stuff on you so it's fine to be touched. A woman gives herself permission to touch your flour 'stains' and point them out to you (as if I don't know they're there). If flour is on your nose or cheek, all the better: innocent touches hold the promises of lost innocence to come."

= DER GASTRO-SEXUAL MANN =

In 2014, German author Carsten Otte published *Der Gastro-Sexual Mann*, a book exploring gastrosexuality. "If I serve you a very special ice cream, a tonka bean ice cream, it melts in your mouth and sends you into raptures," Otte told broadcaster *Deutsche Welle*. "That's what I aim for, and I'm sure you'd say that's a form of sexuality. I call it gastrosexuality, because the way we men cook is more about professional cooking and not what housewives used to do."

GOOD•FEL•LAS THIN

(*noun*): Measurement of a slice of garlic cut paper-thin using a razor blade.

....

= PRISON CUISINE =

The term is a reference to a famous scene in Martin Scorsese's 1990 film *Goodfellas*, in which gangster Henry Hill (Ray Liotta) describes in detail how mob boss Paulie Cicero (Paul Sorvino) prepared dinner while locked up: "In prison, dinner was always a big thing. We had a pasta course, then we had a meat or a fish. Paulie was doing a year for contempt and had a wonderful system for garlic. He used a razor and sliced it so thin it would liquefy in the pan with a little oil. It's a very good system."

≡ ORIGINS ≡

In a foreword to *The Wiseguy Cookbook*, Nicholas Pileggi, author of *Wiseguy* (the book upon which the film *Goodfellas* was based), said that the real-life mobster Henry Hill learned the technique from his mother: "Henry was very proud of the fact that his mother's garlic slicing technique was so well received by his Mob pals that it was enthusiastically taken up by his entire crew doing time in the Italian Mob suites at the Lewisburg Penitentiary in Pennsylvania."

≡ INFLUENCE ≡

Throughout chef Andrew Carmellini's 2008 cookbook *Urban Italian: Simple Recipes and True Stories from a Life in Food*, the recipes repeatedly call for garlic cloves to be sliced "*Goodfellas* thin."

GREASE BAN•DIT

(*noun*): A thief who steals used cooking oil from restaurants.

....

≡ ORIGINS ≡

While used cooking oil has historically had a second life—it can be turned into livestock feed and used in the production of soap and detergents—the advent of biofuels and a robust new market for alternative fuels has led to rising demand for used grease, which can be processed into biodiesel. A black market in stolen grease has emerged, fueled by thefts of used cooking oil from restaurants by criminals dubbed "grease bandits" in a 2008 article in the *Globe and Mail*. The thefts can be difficult to prosecute because law enforcement often equates grease with refuse.

≡ LIQUID GOLD ≡

Demand for biofuels has caused the price of "yellow grease," which is traded on the commodity markets, to increase dramatically. According to the *New York Times*, yellow grease jumped from 7.6 cents per pound in 2000 to 33 cents per pound in 2008.

≡ GREASE MARKET ≡

According to a 2013 article in the *New Yorker*, "an enterprising thief can steal four thousand dollars' worth of grease in half an hour." Grease bandits consider fried chicken chains to be some of the best targets because they change out their grease more frequently and chicken doesn't tend to break up and contaminate the oil, leaving grease with less sediment. According to a 2014 article in the *Dallas Morning News*, grease thefts more than doubled between 2005 and 2012 (when 5,943 grease thefts were reported nationwide) and cost the rendering industry more than $39 million annually.

= LARD OF THE GREASE =

In an episode of *The Simpsons* titled "Lard of the Dance," Homer discovered that he could make a quick profit by stealing and reselling grease but failed at a series of attempts at grease banditry.

GREASE-LOAD·ING

(*noun*): The practice of eating a diet high in fat in preparation for athletic endurance.

....

≡ ORIGINS ≡

While interest in the potential benefits of a diet high in fats and low in carbohydrates dates back decades, the earliest citation for the term *grease-loading* appeared in a 2003 discussion on the Chowhound online food forum on the culinary merits of crab Rangoon and fried cream cheese wontons. Grease-loading reappeared on sports blogs and forums in 2009 as an alternative to carbo-loading. The term was introduced widely to the general public in a 2015 article by Gretchen Reynolds in the *New York Times* on the potential benefits of a high-fat diet for endurance athletes.

≡ SCIENCE ≡

Jeff Volek, a professor in the Department of Human Sciences at Ohio State University in Columbus and an advocate of high-fat diets, argues that humans evolved to eat fat over carbohydrates: "Early humans, the hunter-gatherers, who were quite physically active, primarily ate fat. It's been the main fuel for active humans far longer than carbohydrates have been." To gain the benefits of fat as a fuel for better sports performance, Volek recommends a diet close to 85 percent fat and almost no carbohydrates. Such a diet leads to a condition called ketosis, where the body creates molecules called ketones that will be burned as fuel when the blood lacks sugar.

≡ HISTORY ≡

Canadian Arctic explorer Vilhjalmur Stefansson was an early adopter of low (or no) carbohydrate diets. In 1928, he spent most of the year eating an Inuit diet consisting of 85 percent fat and 15 percent protein under close observation in Bellevue Hospital in New York City without impaired health or any sign of nutritional deficiencies.

≡ ANTONYM ≡

Carbo-load·ing (*noun*): Eating a high carbohydrate diet prior to sports activities.

≡ HOMONYM ≡

Grease-loading also refers to the practice of refilling a grease gun, a tool used for lubrication by automobile mechanics.

GROWL•ETTE (*noun*):
A thirty-two-ounce beer container, typically made of glass, that is half the size of a traditional growler.

....

≡ ORIGINS ≡

According to word sleuth Nancy Friedman's *Fritinancy* blog, one of the earliest references to growlettes dates back to 2011 when the Throwback Brewery in North Hampton, New Hampshire, announced that it was launching diminutive versions of growlers for taking home beer: "These new growlers are very cute 32 oz. flip-tops (approx. ½ the size of our original growler), so we decided to give them a name—'growlettes.' We love these new bottles. They are slim enough so that you can fit several into your fridge without requiring displacement of core food items (although we think beer is a core food item). Given their size, the growlettes will allow you to more easily bring home multiple varieties of beer at a time."

≡ SYNONYM ≡

Growlettes are also known by the name *howlers* (half growlers).

The contemporary growler, a sixty-four-ounce glass or ceramic vessel for transporting draft beer home from a brewery or brewpub, originated as two-quart buckets in the days before bottling. In the run up to Prohibition, open bucket-style growlers came under attack by antialcohol temperance groups and were outlawed in some areas. They eventually evolved into the "Duck," a closed metal flask-like growler that featured a hook to hide the beer from the public and the police by hanging it on the inside underarm of one's coat.

HAUTE BARN·YARD

(*adjective*): A term describing a genre of restaurants that adhere to a highly self-conscious style of rusticity and typically serve a menu with an emphasis on dishes that are local and seasonal.

≡ ORIGINS ≡

New York magazine restaurant critic Adam Platt coined the term in a 2006 review of the Tasting Room: "The windowless dining space in the back is much bigger than that of the original restaurant and decorated in a style that might be described as Haute Barnyard, with a long, communal farm table in the middle of the room, dimly lit booths in the back, and artsy depictions of painted sheep, oversize chicken bones, and giant, sculptural tangerine peels scattered over the brick walls."

HOW TO GO BARNYARD

The essential accoutrements of haute barnyard restaurants, according to Adam Platt:

- At least three varieties of artisanal mushrooms
- Rustic chalkboards
- Herbs in the bathroom ("if you're lucky, a sprig of lavender")

> Communal tables
>
> Heirloom pork
>
> American cheeses
>
> An egg fetish
>
> Pictures of animals on the walls

≡ EDISANAL ≡

The warm glow and vintage look of Edison light bulbs—those carbon filament reproductions of century-old bulbs—are de rigueur for illuminating haute barnyard restaurants. Coffee website Sprudge.com coined the term *Edisanal* in 2014 to capture this lighting trend and its rustic sensibility: "Derived from or directly related to the use of Edison light bulbs in cafes, Edisanal as an approach extends from reclaimed wood bars, to found light fixtures, to a whole world of carefully patinaed Americana."

≡ HOMONYM ≡

A 2015 article in *Out* magazine deployed haute barnyard to describe fashion photo shoots with model Chad White that featured animal themes (he appeared astride a horse, wearing wings, and cuddling a cat): "This isn't the first time the model has appeared in the magazine, but his past cameos have been less haute couture than haute barnyard."

HON•EY
LAUN•DER•ING (*noun*):
Fraud involving trade in tainted honey to skirt U.S. taxes.

....

≡ ORIGINS ≡

The first reports of honey laundering appeared in 2008 amid U.S. government crackdowns on diluted or contaminated honey produced in China, the world's leading exporter of honey, but "laundered" in other countries to disguise its origin and evade U.S. tariffs and inspections. The global scheme included shipments of bad honey through India, Malaysia, Australia, Indonesia, Russia, and Thailand, among other countries.

≡ HONEYGATE ≡

Beginning in 2011, the U.S. Department of Homeland Security started an undercover investigation into Honey Holding, one of the biggest suppliers of honey to U.S. food companies. Dubbed "Project Honeygate," the investigation led to federal indictments of Honey Holding as well as a company called Groeb Farms and several honey brokers, for evading $180 million in tariffs. Five people pleaded guilty to fraud, including one executive at Honey Holding, who was given a six-month prison sentence.

≡ FOOD DETECTIVES ≡

Chemists in U.S. government labs are using sophisticated methods to detect the origin of imported honey. According to a 2015 article in the *New York Times*, the scientists are using a mass spectrometer to measure the amount of chromium, iron, copper, and other elements in honey samples. The unique combination of trace metals reflects the composition of certain soils where flowering plants were foraged by bees. Because soils vary geographically, the data can help determine the country of origin of suspect honey.

≡ DEFINING HONEY ≡

The U.S. honey industry has repeatedly sought a federal standard of identity for honey. The Food and Drug Administration denied a 2011 petition by the honey lobby for a definition of honey, but in 2014, the United States Department of Agriculture issued a call for comments on "how a Federal standard of identity for honey would be in the interest of consumers, the honey industry, and U.S. agriculture."

HY·PER·COOK·ING

(*noun*): An environmentally conscious practice of cooking that seeks to maximize the impact of energy used during the cooking process.

....

≡ ORIGINS ≡

Jackie Newgent, RD, introduced the term in her *Big Green Cookbook* (2009), based on the idea of "hypermiling": "Heard of hypermiling, where you take any advantage you can to conserve gas while driving? Well, you can do the same with cooking."

≡ TECHNIQUES ≡

Newgent offers twenty-seven tips for low-carbon cooking, such as:

+ When using a gas or electric grill, cook food with the grill turned on for part of the time and turned off for the rest to save energy.

+ Choose foods that are thin to begin with—like angel hair pasta instead of fettuccine—that don't need to be cooked as long.

+ Practice "green sautéing" by cooking food in a skillet over a burner only part of the time and using the residual heat in the pan off the burner for the rest of the cooking process.

+ Cut vegetables into smaller pieces before cooking so

that they cook faster and require less cooking time
and energy.

+ Cook food only until "green doneness" (i.e., until it is
safe to eat but cooked no further).

+ Use microwave ovens, which require much less energy
than conventional ovens, more frequently.

≡ HYPERBAKING ≡

When it comes to using the oven, Newgent recommends
"hyperbaking"—placing foods in a cold oven and allowing them to begin baking as the oven preheats—to save on
overall cooking time and reduce the amount of energy use
through traditional baking.

≡ HOMONYM ≡

Diverging from hypercooking as an ecologically minded cook-
ing technique, Sony Computer Entertainment Hong Kong
Limited announced in early 2015 the release of *Dekamori
Senran Kagura*, a PlayStation video game centered around a
"Sexy Hyper Cooking Battle." The game is a spin-off of the
Senran Kagura video game series featuring a team of busty
ninjas doing battle in various states of undress.

HY·PER·PAL·AT·ABLE

(*adjective*): Describes processed foods that have been engineered with precise levels of fat, sugar, flavors, and food additives to stimulate the human brain.

....

═ ORIGINS ═

The concept of hyperpalatable foods was coined by former Food and Drug Administration commissioner Dr. David A. Kessler in his book *The End of Overeating: Taking Control of the Insatiable American Appetite* (2009). It's based on the scientific notion of palatability, which Kessler defines as the "capacity to stimulate the appetite and prompt us to eat more." Hyperpalatability, in turn, is the quality of foods that have been engineered to optimize their palatability: "The combination of sugar and fat is what people prefer, and it's what they'll eat most. The art of pleasing the palate is in large part a matter of combining them in optimal amounts. That can do more than make food palatable. It can make food 'hyperpalatable.'"

═ IRRESISTIBILITY ═

In *The End of Overeating*, Kessler cites a number of hyperpalatable foods with attributes that enhance their "craveability." Here are just a few:

Nacho Cheese Doritos: Three different cheese notes

provide multiple "flavor hits." Salt and oil add to the pleasure of the eating experience, along with distinctive textures—the crunch of the first bite, followed by a meltdown that "turns the chips into a sauce in the mouth."

Cheetos Flamin' Hot: This completely processed product takes eaters on a "roller coaster ride" of cheesy, hot, and spicy flavors and crunchy textures.

Cinnabon cinnamon rolls: Three different kinds of sugar enhance the softness of the dough, the stickiness of the filling, and the creaminess of the frosting, and the warm temperature at which they are served heightens the sensory experience.

≡ FOOD ADDICTION ≡

A 2011 study by researchers at Yale University concluded that "foods, particularly hyperpalatable ones, demonstrate similarities with addictive drugs." Moreover, a 2013 study at Connecticut College found that Oreo cookies were more addictive to lab rats than cocaine. The researchers found that Oreos activated more neurons in the nucleus accumbens (the brain's "pleasure center") than drugs. "This correlated well with our behavioral results and lends support to the hypothesis that high-fat/high-sugar foods are addictive," said Joseph Schroeder, who oversaw the research.

ICE CHEF (*noun*): A bar worker whose responsibility is to oversee the freezing and cutting of numerous types and shapes of ice tailored for use in specific cocktails.

═ ORIGINS ═

An ice chef may be a permanent position or a niche function filled by different staff members at a bar. One of the earliest published references to the role appeared in a 2011 article by Kara Newman on the elaborate ice program at the Aviary in Chicago: "All of the ice is made by Micah Melton, who is alternately known as the ice man, the Eskimo, or the ice chef. 'All he does is freeze things,' [then executive chef Craig] Schoettler says. 'It's a very important job. We don't want this done haphazardly, so we have one guy dedicated to ice.'"

═ ICE MASTER ═

Japanese bartender Hidetsugu Ueno, legendary bartender and ice chef at Tokyo's Bar High Five, is known internationally for his ice-carving mastery, including a "brilliant-cut" faceted ice shape that resembles a giant diamond.

═ FROM SPHERES TO SPEARS ═

Ice chefs use molds, ice machines, and even a range of special knives to create the variety of ice shapes demanded by high-end bars. These are some popular ice shapes used in the craft cocktail world, according to Nick Korn, bartender and beverage industry strategist:

Spheres: Hand-cut or molded ball-shaped ice.

Spears: Either molded or hand-cut from a block, these are roughly 1 by 1 by 5 inches and fit perfectly in a Collins glass.

Cones: Traditionally used in tiki cocktails like the Navy Grog, cones are made from crushed ice pressed in a mold and refrozen, usually with a hole for a straw.

"Sexy ice": Perfect cubes or rough-hewn shapes meant to fit neatly into an old fashioned glass.

Pellet ice: Small bits of ice that are more aesthetically attractive and stable than traditional crushed ice (also known as Scotsman ice for the machine that makes it).

Kold-Draft: The one-and-a-quarter-inch standard cocktail ice, which has become ubiquitous in craft cocktail bars. The shape is named for the Kold-Draft ice machine, though it can be made in other ice machines.

JAN•O•PAUSE (*noun*):

An annual challenge to abstain from drinking during the month of January.

....

≡ ORIGINS ≡

The *Daily Mail* is widely credited with coining the term for this month-long postholiday detox in a 2002 article. The Janopause may also be known as a "Dry January" or "drynuary." In Finland, there is a tradition of the *tipaton tammikuu*, translated as the "dropless January."

≡ PROS ≡

A research study on the health benefits of the Janopause found that volunteers who abstained from drinking for just over five weeks lost 3.3 pounds, lowered their cholesterol levels by 5 percent, and cut blood glucose levels by almost a 25 percent. Cheers to good health!

≡ CONS ≡

On the other hand, doctors warn that abstaining from alcohol for a short period creates a false sense of security and can actually lead people to drink more alcohol once the Janopause is over. "Detoxing for a month is medically futile. It feeds the idea that you can abuse your liver as much as you like and then sort everything with a quick fix," Dr. Mark Wright, a consultant hepatologist at Southampton General Hospital, told the *Times of India*.

"Around the 24th, you catch your first glimpse of the finish line. The goal. The end-game. Suddenly, healthiness, productivity, and abstract notions about being a better human being fall by the wayside. Ahead of you is the only thing that matters: a glass of cool, delicious wine shining so brightly it looks like the Holy Grail."

—ALEX PROUD, COLUMNIST

KO•KU•MI (*noun*): A Japanese word for the taste sensation of thickness, mouthfulness, long-lastingness, and harmony.

≡ ORIGINS ≡

The term is attributed to a 1990 study by Yoichi Ueda and his colleagues at Ajinomoto, a Japanese food and chemical corporation, who found that water extracts of garlic affected the taste of soups. According to food writer and scientist Harold McGee, "the effect was not a distinctive taste of its own, but an increase in qualities that Dr. Ueda called 'continuity, mouthfulness, and thickness,' as well as an overall enhancement of sweetness, saltiness, and umami tastes."

≡ SCIENCE ≡

In a 2010 article in the *Journal of Biological Chemistry*, Japanese scientists published the findings of their research into the causes and mechanisms of the kokumi effect. They found that the presence of certain compounds in food—calcium, protamine (found in milt, or fish sperm, which is eaten in Japan and Russia), L-histidine (an amino acid), and glutathione (found in yeast extract)—caused the kokumi sensation even though they have no taste themselves. For the first time, the researchers demonstrated that the compounds activate flavor enhancement by targeting calcium channels in the tongue.

≡ FIFTH TASTE ≡

Kokumi is related to umami, the so-called fifth taste (after sweet, salty, sour, and bitter), imparted by glutamate and first discovered by Kikunae Ikeda, a professor at Tokyo Imperial University, in 1908.

≡ KOKUMI POWDER ≡

Commercial food producers have sought to capture the kokumi effect by creating food additives that can round out flavors and lessen the need for salt. Japanese firm Nikken Foods makes Komi, a powdered "kokumi ingredient enhancer," and the Israel-based company LycoRed produces SANTE, a kokumi flavor booster marketed to soup makers.

K

LA•ZY FOODS (*noun*): Precut vegetables and other semiprepared foods sold as culinary shortcuts for harried home cooks.

≡ ORIGINS ≡

A 2010 article in the *BBC News Magazine* reported on rising UK supermarket sales of "'lazy food' and cooking 'cheat' ingredients such as peeled potatoes, diced onions, and other partially prepared vegetables that eliminate a step or two in the cooking process."

As reported by the *Telegraph*, a 2010 study of British consumers by the website MySupermarket.co.uk, found that spending on "ready-grated, sliced, and chopped" products was up 14 percent over the previous two years and that women spent 10 percent more on such products than men. Jonny Steel, a MySupermarket spokesman, told the *Telegraph*: "Our great-grandparents would be amazed at the kinds of convenience ingredients sweeping the supermarket shelves—prechopped onions, ready-grated cheese, and even ready-boiled eggs. Foods that were once considered an absurd convenience are now a normal part of our daily routines."

"These ready-prepared ingredients have produced lazy cooks—they think they don't have the time to make real food. But cooking is a bit of ritual, it's a process to start from the beginning with ingredients you prepare yourself. Preparation is an important part of cooking. You get a feel for what you are making. And food tastes better when it's made from scratch."

—LESLEY BALL, HOME ECONOMIST

≡ BOIL YOUR OWN! ≡

Decrying the emergence of preboiled eggs in supermarkets, journalist Oliver Thring called upon Britons to rise up against this ultimate lazy food: "Today, I hatch the Boil Your Own movement. Join me. Stand up for patience, decency, craft, and civilisation. Fight for the yolk of yore, the albumen of Albion. Boil an egg, put it in your child's lunchbox, or in a salad, or go to work on it. Because if you don't act now, my friends, the consequences will be serious. Sure as eggs is eggs."

LEX·I·CAL-
GUS·TA·TO·RY
SYN·ES·THE·SIA (*noun*):

A rare condition that causes individuals to experience a strong sense of taste and smell with certain words.

....

≡ SCIENCE ≡

The neurological phenomenon known as synesthesia typically involves the joining of two or more senses involuntarily. Typically, people with the condition might associate what they see with certain colors (numbers or letters are felt as colors). But scientists have also discovered that some synesthetes experience words as tastes. Three cases were reported in the early 1900s, but a series of studies beginning in 2003 have provided greater insight into this unusual form of synesthesia.

≡ WORD ASSOCIATION ≡

Researchers have observed a number of unusual associations between words and taste in their subjects. Here are a few examples from a study by Jamie Ward of the University College London and Julia Simner of the University of Edinburgh published in the journal *Cognition* in 2003:

WORD	TASTES LIKE
London	potato
union	onions
microscope	carrots
confess	coffee
newspaper	chips
auction	Yorkshire pudding
six	vomit
human	baked beans
April	apricots
safety	buttered toast
jail	bacon

═ TUBE TASTE ═

James Wannerton, who was diagnosed with lexical-gustatory synesthesia, spent forty-nine years creating a flavor map of the London Underground based on the tastes he associated with each station. He named Tottenham Court Road one of the tastiest stops: "This is one of the strongest flavours on the map. It tastes of sausage and egg. There are crusty bits of burnt sausage and the egg is well done. A lovely breakfast taste."

LO·CA·POUR (*noun*): A person who consumes only beer, wine, and spirits that are made locally.

≡ ORIGINS ≡

One of the earliest mentions of locapour, the drinking corollary of a locavore, can be found in a 2008 article on "The Virtues and Pleasures of Being a 'Locapour'" appearing in Canada's *Globe and Mail*: "Then there's the locavore movement—or, in this case, the locapour movement, as one might call it. Environmentally sensitive people are starting to see the virtue of drinking domestic product rather than transoceanic cargo, just as Europeans have done since the dawn of fermented fruit."

≡ GOING LOCAL ≡

A team of researchers from Cornell's Charles H. Dyson School of Applied Economics and Management explored the extent to which restaurants in New York State served wines made locally. The study, published as a working paper by the American Association of Wine Economists, mined the Zagat Survey for data on restaurant cuisine, food quality, decor, and cost combined with additional data on wines offered in fifteen hundred restaurants. "When we looked at all New York state wines, restaurants that serve New American cuisine were far more likely to serve local wines than other cuisines," said assistant professor Brad Rickard. "A focus on natural or organic ingredients and a high Zagat décor rating were also correlated with a willingness to buy local."

≡ LOCAPOUR LINGO ≡

farm-to-bar: New York City's Apothéke touts itself as "the first cocktail bar to adhere to a strict 'Farm-to-Bar' ideology, sourcing the ingredients of our cocktails from local greenmarkets, organic produce venders, and our own Rooftop Herb Garden."

farm-to-barrel: Barrel-aged beers brewed with fruit from local farms. In 2014, San Francisco–based farm-to-barrel brewery Almanac Beer Company released its Valley of Heart's Delight beer made with hand-picked apricots, loquats, and cherries foraged in the nearby Santa Clara Valley.

farm-to-glass cocktail: A cocktail using seasonal fruits and vegetables produced on local farms.

MEAT·MARE (*noun*):

A terrifying dream afflicting some vegetarians in which the dreamer experiences extreme feelings of anxiety about meat.

....

≡ HAUNTED BY BACON ≡

A member of the online forum VeggieBoards recalled a meatmare that involved gorging on bacon: "I had one a few weeks ago. I was on like a hotel balcony just stuffing bacon in my mouth. I could hear my concious [sic] mind telling me not to eat it, that it was bad for me. I also remember my brother in the dream yelling at me from below not to eat it. I made myself wake up and was so happy it was only a dream."

≡ MEAT, DREAMS, AND MUSIC ≡

The Quicksilver Meat Dream (2003) is the fourth album by the Canadian alternative rock band I Mother Earth. "Meatmare" is the first track on John Ward's 2013 album *John Ward's Electric Séance, Vol. 1.*

≡ CARNIVORE'S DILEMMA ≡

The carnivorous creators of the viral web series *EpicMealTime* define meatmares as night terrors induced by the eating of meat: "If you consume ⅛th of the amount of meat that EpicMealTime does in any given week, then of course you know what we're talking about when we say that you have had the 'Meat Sweats' or that you've experienced 'MeatMares.' It's when your bodily fluids are congested with thousands of calories and your blood content is consumed with grease and liquor."

≡ SCROOGED ≡

In *A Christmas Carol*, a disbelieving Ebenezer Scrooge chalks up the image of Jacob Marley's ghost to "an undigested bit of beef," among other foodstuffs. He tells the ghost, "There's more of gravy than of grave about you, whatever you are!"

MEAT STY·LUS (*noun*):

A snack sausage repurposed as an input device for the iPhone's capacitive touch screen.

. . . .

≡ ORIGINS ≡

In 2010, the electronics blog *Engadget* reported that snack sausages were being used as meat styli by South Koreans to operate their iPhones in inclement weather: "Apparently snack sausages from the CJ Corporation are electrostatically compatible with the iPhone's capacitive touch screen, leading many to use them as a 'meat stylus' in the cold weather, rather than remove a glove. And it's not just a joke; apparently South Korean snack sausage sales are soaring." In fact, according to a report on the South Korean news site Inews24.com, sales of CJ Corporation snack sausages went up by 39 percent over the previous year.

≡ "SURPRISINGLY FUN" ≡

CaseCrown, a maker of iPhone cases and other accessories, soon began selling a meat stylus on its website. In a review of the stylus, Gizmodo.com found that the sausage input device was reasonably priced at five dollars and left no fingerprints on the screen. As for typing with the meat stylus, using one sausage was "hell," but typing with two was "surprisingly fun": "When using two sausages, it almost feels normal to gently beat your screen with meat products—like drumming."

≡ SAUSAGE GLOVES ≡

In 2013, the Japanese comedy website Daily Portal Z spoofed the meat stylus meme by creating a "sausage glove" that could be used with smartphones.

M

MINI COWS (*noun*): Diminutive cows, no taller than forty-two inches at maturity, suited for small acreage farms.

≡ SHORT RIBS ≡

As farmers downsize, special breeds of waist-high mini cows are gaining in appeal. As of 2010, according to the *Guardian*, there are more than twenty thousand mini cows in the United States. According to the International Miniature Cattle Breeder's Society, full miniature cows are classified as cattle breeds that are forty-two inches or less at maturity. There are currently twenty-six breeds of mini cows recognized by the organization.

≡ "GREEN" RED MEAT ≡

Mini cows are prized for their environmental benefits over larger cattle. They can be kept on as little as one acre of land, eat one-third the amount of feed, and produce only one-tenth the amount of methane as full-size heifers.

≡ BY THE NUMBERS ≡

While a standard-size milk cow can provide six to ten gallons of milk per day, a mini cow will produce one to one and a half gallons per milking. Moreover, a mini cow, which typically weighs between five hundred and seven hundred pounds, can provide enough meat to feed a family of four for six months.

≡ TEACUPS ≡

The smallest breeds of mini cows, cattle less than thirty-six inches tall, are known as "teacup cattle."

≡ MINI HEIFERS FOR EL JEFE ≡

Former Cuban president Fidel Castro was an early adopter of the mini cow movement. The *Wall Street Journal* reported in 2002 that Castro hoped to develop a breed of tiny dog-sized cows that could be kept by families in their apartments to solve the problem of milk scarcity in Cuban cities. According to Boris Luis Garcia, a molecular biologist who worked on the project for three years, the cows would graze on grass grown in drawers under fluorescent lighting. Alas, the Cuban mini cow project never came to fruition.

MIS•O•PHO•NIA (*noun*):

Literally the "hatred of sound," a condition characterized by the inability to tolerate certain noises, especially chewing.

....

═ ORIGINS ═

The term was introduced by neuroscientists Pawel and Margaret Jastreboff in 2002 to describe a chronic condition in which an individual experiences anxiety, panic, or rage when they hear certain sounds such as lip smacking, chewing, and crunching. Misophonia's causes are unknown, and there is a debate over whether it constitutes a psychiatric disorder or a neurological dysfunction. Current treatments typically consist of group therapy based on cognitive behavioral techniques.

═ TRIGGERS ═

According to Misophonia Online (misophonia.com), the following sounds may trigger a misophonic response: "ahhs" after drinking, burping, chewing, crunching (ice or other hard food), gulping, gum chewing and popping, silverware scraping teeth or a plate, slurping, sipping, licking, smacking, spitting, sucking (ice, etc.), swallowing, talking with food in one's mouth, tooth sucking, lip smacking, wet mouth sounds, grinding teeth, throat clearing, and jaw clicking.

In 2015, the *New York Times* solicited feedback from

misophonia sufferers about their most unbearable sounds. One in four readers complained that soup slurping was intolerable, while 18 percent could not abide the snapping sound of gum chewing.

≡ THE POPCORN CURE ≡

Sitting in a movie theater surrounded by people chomping on popcorn can be insufferable for misophones. Paul Tabachnek, who lives with the condition, told the *New Republic* in 2013 that he wears padded headphones in cinemas to dampen the sound of crunching kernels.

≡ CELEBS ≡

In 2011, television personality Kelly Ripa revealed she suffered from misophonia. She told ABC News, "When my husband eats a peach, I need to leave the room."

MOM WINES (*noun*): Wines that appeal to busy mothers for their ready availability, familiarity, and modest prices.

....

≡ ORIGINS ≡

Writing for *Bon Appétit* in 2014, Danielle Walsh recounted her brush with mom wines at a Brooklyn steakhouse: "I saw something on the wine list that I never expected to see: Pinot Grigio. Not only was this a strange choice for a steakhouse—a wimpy white for a caveman-caliber piece of meat?—but this wine list was also pretty hip. Which, well, Pinot Grigio just...isn't. It's thin, sometimes too fruit-forward, lacking in character, and often tastes mass-produced. Like some $7 White Zinfandel or a super buttery Chardonnay, it's what I thought of as 'mom wine.'"

≡ MOMS NEED WINE ≡

Marile Borden, a mother of two from Boston, created the "Moms Who Need Wine" Facebook page (with more than seven hundred thousand likes) and website in 2009 as a "personal experiment": "You're trying to cook dinner and help your 7-year-old with homework, your 4-year-old wants a snack... Sometimes you need to kick your feet up and have a glass of wine."

≡ LITERATURE ≡

Stefanie Wilder-Taylor, a blogger, stand-up comic, and mother of three, tapped into the mom wine trend with two wine-themed parenting books, *Sippy Cups Are Not for Chardonnay* (2006) and *Naptime Is the New Happy Hour* (2008). In 2009, she announced she had a drinking problem and gave up alcohol.

≡ MOMMY WARS ≡

In 2011, California-based winery Clos LaChance Wines filed a federal lawsuit to declare that its brand MommyJuice Wines does not violate the trademark of a competitor, Mommy's Time Out. "Mommy is a generic word that they don't have a monopoly on," said KC Branch, an attorney representing Clos LaChance.

"Above all else, wine should be fun, relaxing, and something you can afford to look forward to at the end of each and every day. This is your time. Time to enjoy a moment to yourself. A moment without the madness."

—MAD HOUSEWIFE CELLARS, PRODUCER OF MOM WINES

NAN•O•BREW•ERY

(*noun*): A scaled-down microbrewery, often run by a solo entrepreneur, that produces beer in small batches.

═ ORIGINS ═

One of the first reports on the mini microbrewing trend, a 2009 article on MSN.com, suggested that nanobrewing had emerged as part of the larger trend toward locavorism: "For years, microbrewers—independent beer-brewing operations whose threshold of production is less than 15,000 barrels a year—defined the small-batch experience. More recently, though, the drive for local identities and products, and a reawakening of Americans' sense of the neighborhood as resource, have led to the rise of nanobreweries, run by a handful of people operating out of very limited neighborhood spaces on a very limited budget."

Delaware-based craft brewer Dogfish Head may have been the original nanobrewery when it was founded in 1996. Founder Sam Calagione says Dogfish was "nano before nano was cool."

═ NANO-MAGIC ═

Tapping into the nanobrewery phenomenon, SABCO, a commercial brewing equipment supplier, brought to market specialized gear downsized for the needs of diminutive brewing operations. SABCO touted its two-barrel Nano-Magic brewing system, launched in 2012, as "ideal for a brew-pub or nano-brewery environment."

≡ TRENDING ≡

Hess Brewing Company, which calls itself "San Diego's first nanobrewery," defines a nanobrewery as a beer-making operation that produces less than three barrels per batch. As of 2012, it counted more than ninety nanobreweries in operation in the United States, with more than fifty in the planning stages.

≡ MICRODISTILLERIES ≡

Just as microbreweries have spawned nanobreweries, liquor companies have spawned microdistilleries, boutique producers of spirits made in small quantities.

NOM·MU·NI·CA·TION

(*noun*): A hybrid Japanese English word describing the informal social discourse that takes place between coworkers while drinking after-hours.

≡ ORIGINS ≡

Roughly translated as "drinkcommunication," the word is a contraction of the Japanese word *nomu* (to drink) and *communication*.

≡ SOCIAL LUBRICATION ≡

Drinking among workmates encourages a sense of team spirit and togetherness called *soshikiryoku*, which is an important part of Japanese business culture. Moreover, in a hierarchical Japanese working environment, drinking outside of the office affords an alternative space where two-way communication is possible between senior and junior colleagues.

≡ HOMAGE ≡

In 2009, the restaurant chain Umami Burger opened a Japanese-themed bar named Salaryman on Hollywood Boulevard in Los Angeles. According to Urbandaddy.com, "The name is Eastern slang for a working stiff, so think of it more like an illicit drown-your-sorrows watering hole, where you can pull up a stool starting at 11 a.m. for an oversized bottle of Echigo Rice Lager, a Coedo Sweet Potato Beer, or a Hitachino."

≡ FACTS ≡

According to 2014 statistics compiled by the World Health Organization, Japanese adults drink 7.2 liters of alcohol per year per capita on average, exceeding the global average of 6.2 liters by 16 percent.

"Traditionally, the consumption of alcohol has been the Japanese cultural signal that it's ok to be frank and open. The natural loosening of inhibitions from alcohol also has the effect of loosening lips. After-work bonding over alcohol thus also creates the perfect atmosphere for getting things out on the table that are too hard to say while in the constrained environment of the office."

—ROCHELLE KOPP, MANAGING PRINCIPAL,
JAPAN INTERCULTURAL CONSULTING

NUT RAGE (*noun*):
An angry reaction to nuts served in an improper manner.

═ ORIGINS ═

Nut rage refers to a 2014 incident in which Cho Hyun-ah, a former Korean Air vice president, berated an airline employee for serving nuts improperly and then forced the plane to return to the departure gate so that the chief flight attendant could be kicked off. Cho reportedly forced him to kneel and jabbed him with a service manual while demanding he apologize.

═ NUTIQUETTE ═

At the heart of the controversy was Cho's indignation when the flight attendant gave her an unopened bag of macadamia nuts—without first asking if she wanted them—and failed to serve them on a plate per Korean Air service rules.

═ MACADAMIA FRENZY ═

The controversy prompted Koreans to go, well, nuts for macadamias. According to *Korea JoongAng Daily*, sales of macadamia nuts from Hawaiian nut company Mauna Loa jumped by a whopping 2,505 percent in South Korea during the days following the incident.

≡ NUT CRIME ≡

After resigning and apologizing for her nut rage, Cho was jailed and went on trial in January 2015. A South Korean judge sentenced her to one year in prison, ruling that she violated aviation law, changed a flight path, and interfered with operations. She was freed in May 2015 after an appeals court ruled she did not cause a change in the flight path and suspended her sentence.

≡ COMEUPPANCE ≡

Cho is the forty-year-old heiress of the Hanjin Group, which owns Korean Air and is one of South Korea's large family-controlled conglomerates or *chaebol* ("money clan"). Writing in the *Atlantic* in 2015, Devin DeCiantis and Ivan Lansberg maintained that her "'Nut Rage' fed into the worst stereotypes of capitalist privilege." They argued that that the media's intense scrutiny of Cho's sense of entitlement and the public outrage over her behavior was an expression of popular resentment toward the rich and powerful *chaebol*.

N

NU·TRI·COS·MET·ICS

(*noun*): Cosmetic products made from food that are designed to beautify skin, hair, and nails.

═ ORIGINS ═

Ake Dahlgren, a Swedish biochemist who launched the Imedeen brand of skin care products in the 1980s, is considered to be the founder of nutricosmetics. Demand for food-based beauty products has grown steadily since their introduction. According to *Nutraceuticals World*, global sales of nutricosmetics reached $4.5 billion in 2011, mostly in China and Japan. A 2015 analysis by Global Industry Analysts predicted that global sales will increase to $7.4 billion by 2020, with the United States emerging as the world's fastest growing market.

═ BEAUTY YOGURT ═

Danone launched its Essensis yogurt in 2007, promising better skin via a proprietary blend called ProNutris containing vitamin E, green tea–derived antioxidants, probiotics, and borage oil. After failing to take hold in the marketplace, the "dermo-nutrition" product was pulled in France in 2009. *New Nutrition Business* magazine blamed the supermarket retail setting for poor sales: "That's not a place where a brand can acquire any cachet or mystique."

≡ "LUBE FOR YOUR BODY" ≡

Designer Norma Kamali sells two hundred milliliter bottles of olive oil, which she calls "liquid gold," for fifty-eight dollars online. "Consuming olive oil is like having a lube for your body," Kamali told the *New York Times* in 2011. "You are like a well-oiled machine when you consume olive oil."

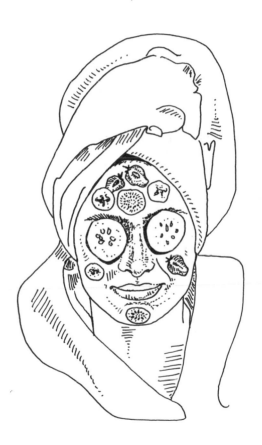

ORTH•OREX•IA NER•VO•SA (*noun*):

A pathological obsession with avoiding the consumption of unhealthy foods.

....

≡ ORIGINS ≡

The term derives from the Greek *orthos* ("right" or "correct") and *orexis* ("appetite"). It was coined in 1997 by Steven Bratman, MD, coauthor of *Health Food Junkies: Orthorexia Nervosa: Overcoming the Obsession with Healthful Eating* (2001). Although orthorexia is not recognized as a mental disorder by the American Psychiatric Association, Bratman has claimed that the fixation on avoiding unhealthy foods can lead to malnutrition and even death. It is closely related to obsessive-compulsive disorder.

≡ VEGAN REDUX ≡

In 2014, Jordan Younger, creator of the *Blonde Vegan* blog, declared that she had the eating disorder. "I started suffering from orthorexia," Younger told *People* magazine. "I restricted myself from certain foods—even some that fell under the vegan umbrella—because they were not 100 percent clean or 100 percent raw. I was following thousands of rules in my head that were making me sick." Younger has since modified her diet and renamed her blog the *Balanced Blonde*.

≡ SCIENCE ≡

In 2005, a group of researchers in Italy published an article in *Eating and Weight Disorders* on their work to validate a questionnaire for the diagnosis of orthorexia nervosa. The test comprised fifteen questions, including:

+ When you go in a food shop, do you feel confused?

+ Are your eating choices conditioned by your worry about your health status?

+ Does the thought about food worry you for more than three hours a day?

+ Do you allow yourself any eating transgressions?

+ Do you feel guilty when transgressing?

+ Do you think your mood affects your eating behavior?

+ Do you think that the conviction to eat only healthy food increases self-esteem?

PAS·SIVE DRINK·ING

(*noun*): The secondary, collateral effects of one person's drinking on the well-being of others.

....

≡ ORIGINS ≡

The term borrows from the concepts of secondhand smoke and passive smoking in order to shift the notion of alcohol abuse as an individual problem to one with harmful indirect costs, ranging from miscarriage to car accidents.

According to Worldwidewords.com, the neologism has been around since 1988 as a parody of passive smoking. However, in 2004, Eurocare, a nongovernmental organization, used the concept in a campaign to call attention to the impact of alcohol use on others: "Alcohol not only harms the user, but those surrounding the user, including the unborn child, children, family members, and the sufferers of crime, violence, and drunk-driving accidents: this can be termed environmental alcohol damage or 'passive drinking.'" It was brought into the mainstream in 2009, when Liam Donaldson, the UK's chief medical officer, warned that the secondary damage on individuals and societies caused by alcohol abuse constituted "passive drinking."

"In contrast to smoking, alcohol is too often viewed as a problem for individuals rather than for society. This is not the case. The second-hand effects of alcohol consumption which I collectively term 'passive drinking' are more complex in their causation than those of passive smoking, and more wide-ranging in their impact."

—LIAM DONALDSON, CHIEF MEDICAL OFFICER

= POLICY =

Donaldson's chief recommendations to stem passive drinking were setting a minimum price per unit of alcohol and tightening licensing laws so local authorities had to consider the deaths and health consequences of alcohol in their areas before granting new licenses for pubs.

POT WINE (*noun*): Wine infused with marijuana.

═ ORIGINS ═

According to Michael Steinberger, writing in the *Daily Beast* in 2012, pot wines were a novelty in the 1980s, when they were typically made with rosé wines. He reported that marijuana-laced wines were making a comeback, with a trend toward robust reds (namely cabernet sauvignon and syrah) as the new wines of choice for pot infusions.

═ "FULL BODY BUZZ" ═

CBS News reported in 2014 that singer Melissa Etheridge had partnered with the owners of Greenway Compassionate Relief, a medical marijuana dispensary in Santa Cruz, California, to produce a line of "cannabis-infused fine wines." Due to legal restrictions, Etheridge may only call them "wine tinctures." She recounted the sensation of drinking her pot wine: "You feel a little buzzed from the alcohol and then get a delicious full body buzz."

HOW TO MAKE POT WINE

According to Steinberger, "The recipe for pot wine, such as it is, consists of dropping one pound of marijuana into a cask of fermenting wine, which yields about 1.5 grams of pot per

P

bottle; the better the raw materials—grapes and dope—the better the wine." On the other hand, Matthew Kronsberg, writing for *Gourmet Live* in 2011, chronicled the technique used by "Henry," a James Beard Award–winning chef who preferred not to use his real name: "Recently he made a Riesling (unusual, in that most pot-infused wines are reds), mixing about an ounce of fairly dry (as opposed to fresh) marijuana ("I wanted less of a piney-oily texture") with the wine in a 5-gallon carboy."

WINE
420 RESERVE
Signature

ALC. 14% BY VOL.
750ml

"I don't think most traditional sommeliers will be interested in this for a long time, because they'll see it as somehow impure. And I understand that, but there's going to be some hip, young, cool person who will see the potential."

—MELISSA ETHERIDGE, MUSICIAN
AND POT WINE ENTHUSIAST

P

PREG·OREX·IA

(*noun*): Eating disorder behaviors experienced by women while pregnant such as extreme dieting, obsessive exercise, and bingeing and purging.

....

≡ ORIGINS ≡

One of the earliest references to the term, a combination of *pregnancy* and *anorexia*, dates to 2007, though *New York* magazine published an article, "The Perfect Little Bump," as early as 2004, documenting the obsession among some New York expecting mothers to stay thin throughout their pregnancies.

≡ TREATMENT ≡

In 2014, Timberline Knolls Residential Treatment Center, a residential facility located just outside of Chicago for treating eating disorders, substance abuse, and mood, launched "Lift the Shame," the first web-based support group of its kind specifically targeted to offer support and resources to pregnant women and mothers with eating disorders.

≡ SCIENCE ≡

While pregorexia is not a formally recognized medical diagnosis and there are no statistics on how many pregnant women experience eating disorders, 30 percent of American women don't gain enough weight during pregnancy, according to Dr. Ovidio Bermudez, the chief medical officer at the Eating Recovery Center in Denver, Colorado.

≡ CELEBRITY PREGOREXIA ≡

Excessive media attention to celebrity mothers and weight gained during pregnancy and lost after birth have been blamed by critics for provoking eating disorders in pregnant women. "Between 2003 and 2005, the number of baby-related, baby weight–related covers on tabloids doubled and since then, it's almost become an expectation now that if a celebrity is pregnant, there will be a mention of her body during pregnancy and then there's the countdown to how fast she's going to get the weight off," said Claire Mysko, spokeswoman for the National Eating Disorders Association and coauthor of the book *Does this Pregnancy Make Me Look Fat?*

P

RA•O•TA (*noun*): A Japanese term for people obsessed with ramen noodle soup.

≡ NOODLEHEADS ≡

Raota is a mash-up of *ramen*, the Japanese noodle soup, and the Japanese word *otaku*, slang for people with all-consuming interests (typically fetishizing anime, manga, or video games). These noodle geeks pore over the pages of *Ramen Walker* magazine and search out the very best places to fill their bellies with ramen.

≡ OTAKU SOUTH ≡

Chef Sarah Gavigan, a self-described "white Sicilian cracker from Columbia, Tennessee," named her Nashville pop-up *izakaya* and ramen shop Otaku South: "We begin with RAMEN. Possibly the ultimate comfort food. Go ahead, Google it, and what you will find are fanatics of this magical bowl of broth and noodles. The Japanese call them OTAKU...the obsessed."

≡ THE END OF RAMEN ≡

In a 2015 essay for *Lucky Peach*, chef and restaurateur David Chang, who played a major role in popularizing ramen in the United States when he opened his Momofuku Noodle Bar in New York City in 2004, decried the current state of ramen: "In Japan, ramen was always a fringe pursuit. As with music or literature, the 'cool' food was made by outsiders fighting against the mainstream, because they didn't feel like the mainstream was good enough… But now ramen is everywhere, and a lot of it is the same. I don't want to go to every city and taste the same fucking thing."

≡ HOMONYM ≡

Raota should not be confused with RAOTA, the Radio Amateur Old Timers' Association.

RE•CES•SI•PES (*noun*):

Cost-saving recipes for preparing meals in a recession economy, most likely prepared by a recessionista.

....

≡ ORIGINS ≡

The neologism emerged on several blogs (Recessipes. blogspot.com and Recessionrecipe.blogspot.com) at the tail end of the 2007–2009 recession. As unemployment spiked nationwide, CNN featured a report on "recession recipes" and the Food Network launched a special page dedicated to budget-friendly menu ideas. A 2009 press release from Scripps Networks, the parent company of the Food Network, said: "Check out tons of recession-time recipes ("recessipes") such as a Spanish-style tortilla with eggs or homemade gnocchi in spicy tomato sauce. It doesn't get any cheaper than potatoes, and they're always in season!"

≡ DOWNTURN DELICACIES ≡

As the U.S. economy faltered, the *New York Times* reported that sales were up in 2008 for dried beans and vegetables (+1 percent), frozen pot pies (+23 percent), and frozen side dishes (+48 percent). Sales of macaroni and cheese and SPAM were experiencing robust growth, and sales were "growing, if not booming" for Velveeta.

≡ DEPRESSIPES ≡

Recessipes have their roots in Depression-era cooking. The web series *Great Depression Cooking with Clara*, featuring the late Clara Cannucciari, launched in 2007 with a series of videos documenting recipes made by Cannucciari's mother during the Great Depression. The popular cooking show attracted more than two million views, and a book compiling her budget-minded delicacies, *Clara's Kitchen*, was published in 2009.

≡ RECESSIONISTA ≡

Slow economic growth and high unemployment prompted not only a rethinking of recipes geared toward smaller wallets, but also a rebranding of style mavens as *recessionistas*, frugal fashionistas in search of chic but cheap clothing and beauty products.

SAFE•TY WINE (*noun*):

A wine that is preferred for its consistency and predictability, particularly when choosing a wine sold by the glass.

....

≡ ORIGINS ≡

Safety wines are the wines you choose when you can't be bothered with a long wine list, when you're feeling risk averse, or when you crave something familiar and reliable. They are the comfort foods of wine.

The earliest reference to the term comes from wine writer Alder Yarrow, who wrote in 2008 on his blog *Vinography* about selecting a safety wine, 2004 Château du Rouët Cuvée Belle Poule Blanc: "When I found myself dining alone the other night, and not wanting to think much about which white wine I wanted, I reached for a safety wine. I had never had it before, but I knew it was: white, a blend of different grapes, French, and it was from Provence."

In a 2010 *Wall Street Journal* article titled "A 'Safety Wine' Around the World," wine writer Lettie Teague reported on the resurgence of Sauvignon Blanc and its popularity as a safety wine. Teague wrote of her friend Kim's safety wine selection: "He liked Sauvignon Blanc because, he said, it was lively and refreshing and above all consistent. Sauvignon Blanc, in short, was his safety drink."

≡ DOOMSDAY WINE ≡

Upping the ante on safety wines, episode 11 of season 1 of National Geographic Channel's reality series *Doomsday Preppers* featured a survivalist using the pseudonym Mr. Wayne who was making his own wine on a three-acre orchard to be used for bartering in a potential doomsday scenario involving a global financial takeover by China.

≡ WINE SAFETY ≡

According to the American Academy of Ophthalmology, sparkling wine corks fly up to fifty miles an hour while exiting a bottle and can cause serious injury. Dr. Arthur Willis, clinical associate professor of ophthalmology at Baylor College of Medicine, told *Wine Spectator* in 2011 that an airborne cork could potentially cause eye bleeding, retinal detachment, iris damage, and even blindness. A 2004 British study found that between 1982 and 1999, 20 percent of "bottle related eye trauma" in the U.S. was caused by sparkling wine corks.

S

SEL·ME·LIER (*noun*):

A culinary professional who specializes in salt and its uses in cooking and pairing with food and wine.

. . . .

≡ ORIGINS ≡

Coined by Mark Bitterman, author of *Salted: A Manifesto on the World's Most Essential Mineral, with Recipes* and owner of the Meadow, a gourmet shop in Portland, Oregon, that specializes in salt, *selmelier* is a mash-up of *sel*, the French word for salt, and *sommelier*, a wine steward.

≡ RULES ≡

The five rules of "strategic salting," according to selmelier Mark Bitterman:

1. Eat all the salt you want, as long as you are the one doing the salting.
2. Skew the use of salt toward the end of food preparation.
3. Use only natural, unrefined salts.
4. Make salting a deliberate act.
5. Use the right salt at the right time.

"This may sound like hyperbole, but sprinkle the parchment-fine flakes of Maldon sea salt on homegrown butter leaf lettuce dressed in macerated shallot vinaigrette and you will experience a chlorophyll dynamo of flavor that seems to strum at the very heart of nature. Patter the pink flesh of fresh-caught trout with the stratified lacework flakes of Halen Môn and brace yourself against the sure compulsion to make offerings of hecatombs and burnt flesh to the sea god Poseidon."

—MARK BITTERMAN, SELMELIER

≡ SOME OTHER SOMMS ≡

The word *selmelier* is, of course, rooted in *sommelier*, the name for an expert in wine and pairings of food and wine. Over the years, the term has been adapted to serve many niche tastes:

Beer sommelier

Cheese sommelier
(also known as a
maître fromager)

Music sommelier

Mustard sommelier

Sake sommelier

Soda sommelier

Tea sommelier

Vegetable sommelier

Water sommelier

SHED•IS•TA (*noun*):

An indie winemaker who produces wines in a backyard shed or other low-budget wine-making operation.

....

≡ ORIGINS ≡

Writer Jay McInerny is credited with introducing the term in his Uncorked column for *House & Garden* magazine. In his 2006 collection of essays, *A Hedonist in the Cellar: Adventures in Wine*, McInerny explored the shedista phenomenon in Santa Barbara, California: "The typical Santa Barbara shedista narrative goes like this: you start working in the cellar of a bigger winery and learn the ropes: the region, the vineyards, and the growers. Eventually you borrow from relatives and max out your credit cards to rent a shed, buy a few tanks and a few tons of Syrah, design a label, and make your own wine. You share equipment and wine notes with friends. And you keep your day job in the meantime."

≡ GARAGISTAS ≡

"Garagistas" (or *garagistes*) are French winemakers in the Bordeaux region who produce *vins de garage* ("garage wine"). The garagistas emerged in the 1990s in reaction to the traditional style of making red Bordeaux wine. Of the first garage wines produced in 1991, *Decanter* magazine noted, "The precepts for a garage wine had been laid: viticultural precision, low yield, small-volume, tailor-made winemaking, new oak, and the absence, at least initially, of terroir. The coining of the term 'garage' implied a limited output and a 'where needs must' approach to production."

≡ HOMONYM ≡

Writer Debra Prinzing, the author of seven books on gardening and a self-described shedista, is not a winemaker but an unabashed shed lover. The author of *Stylish Sheds and Elegant Hideaways* (2008), Prinzing defines a shedista as "a person who creates and occupies a small-scale shelter in the garden for personal enjoyment and the pursuit of any creative passion."

SHMEAT (*noun*): In vitro meat grown in a laboratory as an alternative to slaughtering animals.

··

≡ ORIGINS ≡

The word *shmeat*—sheets of meat grown in the laboratory—is attributed to Dr. Vladimir Mironov, a biologist who has pioneered research into the creation of in vitro meat. According to a 2008 NPR report, "Vladimir Mironov, a biologist at the Medical University of South Carolina, is among a handful of scientists culturing meat from animal tissue. His work involves turning formless, textureless patches of the stuff into [a] mass-produced form—like meat sheets, or what one might affectionately call 'shmeat.'"

≡ CULTURED BURGER ≡

In 2013, vascular physiologist Mark Post of the University of Maastricht in the Netherlands created the world's first lab-grown burger: a five-ounce patty made from bovine muscle stem cells cultured in petri dishes. According to the three people who tasted it, "the burger was dry and a bit lacking in flavor." The two-year project to make the burger cost $325,000 and was paid for by Sergey Brin, one of the founders of Google.

≡ CELEBRITY SALAMI ≡

In 2014, a web outfit calling itself BiteLabs.org launched a ruse on social media that it would grow "meat from celebrity tissue samples and use it to make artisanal salami." BiteLabs envisioned a salami cultured from the cells of actor James Franco thusly: "The Franco salami must be smoky, sexy, and smooth. Franco's meat will pair with lean, strong venison. Sharp Tellicherry peppercorns and caramelized onions provide Franco's underlying flavors, complemented by a charming hint of lavender. The Franco salami's taste will be arrogant, distinctive, and completely undeniable."

≡ PREDICTING THE FUTURE ≡

In his 1931 essay "Fifty Years Hence," Winston Churchill imagined a shmeat-filled future: "We shall escape the absurdity of growing a whole chicken in order to eat the breast or wing, by growing these parts separately under a suitable medium."

SMU•SHI (*noun*): Bite-sized squares of bread topped with ingredients such as meat, fish, cheese, or vegetables.

═ ORIGINS ═

Smushi was first introduced in 2007 at the Royal Smushi Café in Copenhagen. The dish is a blend of sushi and *smørrebrød*, the traditional Danish open-faced sandwich—itself a combination of two words, *smørre* ("butter") and *brød* ("bread")—consisting of a slice of buttered dark rye bread topped with meat or fish, cheese, and vegetables.

═ SMØRREBRØD REINVENTED ═

Historically, smørrebrød was considered a humble food of the working class—an inexpensive lunch item that was anything but refined. "I think the sandwich tradition had become excessively fatty and meaty, different kinds of meats stacked, few quality products, few vegetables, no herbs, too little fish, and maybe a little general sloppiness—too little craftsmanship and too many pre-prepared ingredients," Danish chef Adam Aamann told Denmark.de of the usual smørrebrød.

Using quality fish, meats, and condiments, Aamann helped pioneer a rethinking of smørrebrød. The Royal Smushi Café took the trend one step further in transforming the humble open-faced sandwich into a high-end dish with creative ingredients, textural contrasts, and the precise presentation of sushi.

≡ DOWNSIZING ≡

Copenhagen company Danish Minies (danishmini.dk) one-upped Royal Smushi Café with an ultracompact canapé-size version. One might call them "microsmushi."

≡ FULL CIRCLE ≡

The experiment in Japanese Danish fusion cuisine came full circle in 2010 when the Royal Smushi Café opened a branch in Tokyo's Ginza district.

"I felt that it was time for a change because smørrebrød as you would have it served in various places in Copenhagen is actually a very large sandwich. I just thought why not do it smaller? Why not put a little more artistic touch to it?"

—RUD CHRISTIANSEN, OWNER, ROYAL SMUSHI CAFÉ

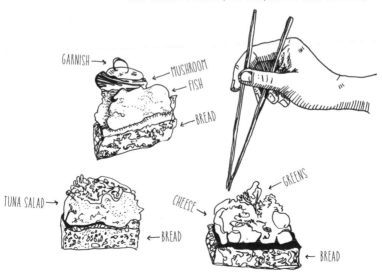

SNACK•I•FY (*verb*): Food industry term for the process of transforming beverages into snack-like food products.

....

≡ ORIGINS ≡

In 2010, Indra Nooyi announced that PepsiCo had purchased Russian dairy and juice maker Wimm-Bill-Dann with the goal of developing products like kefir, a yogurt-like drink that straddles the line between solid snacks and liquid beverages: "We see the emerging opportunity to 'snackify' beverages and 'drinkify' snacks as the next frontier in food and beverage convenience."

"Some say America's become fat and lazy, and we no longer innovate. Well, that is nonsense. We are constantly innovating in the field of fat and lazy... We may finally achieve John F. Kennedy's dream of a chuggable pretzel."

—STEPHEN COLBERT, TELEVISION HOST

≡ IN BETWEEN ≡

In early 2011, Tropicana, a subsidiary of PepsiCo, began a trial launch of Tropolis, a snackified fruit product. According to the *Daily Mail*, "Tropolis, an 80-calorie fruit puree, is considered thick enough to be a snack rather than a beverage and is being marketed at mothers and children."

═ SOCIETAL SNACKIFICATION ═

In a 2014 op-ed article in the *Los Angeles Times*, Daniel Akst used the term to lament the "snackification of everything," from the ubiquity of snack-size foods to texting to bite-sized online journalism. "We gravitate toward snacks because they're fast, easy, and require little commitment," wrote Akst. "They also taste good. Online, snackable items are easily digested by grazing readers, and just as easily shared—the way we once shared meals. In keeping with our demand for flexibility and immediate gratification, snacks are always available, require little investment, and can be consumed without the time and consideration that used to go into more primitive forms of nourishment, such as sit-down dinners or books."

SNACK·WAVE (*noun*):

An Internet trend among young women and teenage girls who incorporate an obsession with snack products and fast foods into their online personas.

≡ ORIGINS ≡

Writing in 2014 at Thehairpin.com, Hazel Cills and Gabrielle Noone coined *snackwave* to describe the phenomenon whereby young women construct an Internet presence using snack foods and fast foods. "It's the antithesis to kale-ridden health food culture and the rise of Pinterest-worthy twee cupcake recipes," wrote Cills and Noone. "Snackwave is defined by exaggeration and extremism. You don't just eat cheeseburgers. You wear a shirt covered in them. You don't just eat pizza. You run a blog devoted to collecting pictures of celebrities eating pizza."

≡ POPWAVE ≡

Pop singers Katy Perry and Miley Cyrus have both incorporated snackwave into their stage acts. Katy Perry used massive balloons of french fries, tacos, and ice cream in both the music video and tour performance for her song "This Is How We Do," and Cyrus rode a giant hot dog over crowds during her Bangers tour.

≡ FOOD FASHION ≡

Designers have tapped into the snackwave meme with fast-food-inspired clothing. Jeremy Scott debuted a collection of dresses printed with packaging images from Fruit Loops, Hershey chocolate bars, and Cheez-It snack crackers for Moschino at the spring 2014 Milan Fashion Week. A snack-wave pioneer, Scott launched his "Food Fight" collection in 2006, featuring outfits emblazoned with french fries, burgers, pizzas, and other foodstuffs.

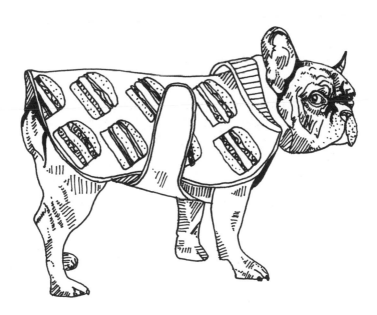

SOME·WHERE·NESS

(*noun*): A term for the unique character found in wines that reflects a specific sense of place.

≡ ORIGINS ≡

Wine writer Matt Kramer coined the term in his 1992 book *Making Sense of California Wine*: "For the first time, it is possible, however tentatively, to start to chart 'somewhereness' in California wines—a familial similarity derived from place."

≡ TERROIR ≡

The concept of somewhereness is linked to that of *terroir*, the French term that describes those characteristics of geography, geology, and climate of a certain place that influence and shape a wine. Over the years, the terroir concept has extended beyond wine making and come to be used in relation to the production of spirits, artisan cheese, coffee, tea, chocolate, and other foodstuffs.

≡ MARKETING ≡

In 2011, Canadian vintner Charles Baker Wines registered *somewhereness* as a trademark. A group of a dozen Ontario winemakers, including Charles Baker Wines, banded together to promote their wines under the somewhereness banner. According to their website, Somewhereness .com, "we've invoked Somewhereness as a word enabling us to articulate in one collective voice. It speaks of small plots, sustainable practices, responsible stewardship, and the way our approach to winemaking contributes to the elusive characteristics that flow through to your soul with every sip of our wine."

═ HISTORY ═

Well before *somewhereness* became a wine term, author Warwick Deeping used it in his 1928 novel *Old Pybus* to describe being in the presence of God: "Mary Merris had found it good to shed tears in this little, funny old room, wherein an old man who had looked on life had brought into being a beautiful faith in the essential somewhereness of God."

S

SOUR·DOUGH HO·TEL (*noun*): A place of lodging for sourdough starters—live cultures of fermented flour, water, and wild yeasts— where they are looked after while their owners go on vacation.

≡ ORIGINS ≡

The only known sourdough hotel in the world can be found in Stockholm at the Urban Deli. Here, customers pay three hundred Swedish krona (about thirty-five dollars) per week at its *surdegshotell* (sourdough hotel) where sourdough starters are maintained with daily "feedings" of flour and water. The hotel holds up to thirty jars of starter, and the top shelf is labeled the penthouse.

≡ HISTORY ≡

Sourdough is believed to have originated in Ancient Egypt around 1500 BC. It remained the typical form of leavening until the Middle Ages, when it was replaced by barm, a product of the beer brewing process, and, eventually, cultured yeasts.

≡ ETERNAL BREAD ≡

With careful maintenance, sourdough can live for years and years. While there is no Guinness World Record for the oldest sourdough, Lucille Dumbrill of Newcastle, Wyoming, claims to have kept alive a starter passed down to her by her mother that has lasted for more than 120 years.

San Francisco has continually produced sourdough bread since 1849, and some bakeries there can trace their starters back to California's gold rush era. The city is so closely associated with sourdough that the dominant strain of lactobacillus in starters was named *Lactobacillus sanfranciscensis*.

═ EUREKA ═

"Sourdough" was a nickname for California Klondike miners because they carried the starter with them to make bread while prospecting.

SPOOF·U·LAT·ED

(*adjective*): A descriptor for wines that have been dramatically manipulated with additives and other modern wine-making technologies that transform flavor, texture, and aroma.

═ ORIGINS ═

The term was popularized by wine importer Harmon Skurnik to characterize wines suffering from overmanipulation. Skurnik recalled first learning of the word in 1990 from a tasting room employee at Chateau Montelena Winery in Napa Valley: "As we tasted through their wines, the pretty young girl behind the counter explained to us how Montelena's Chardonnay did not go through malolactic [fermentation], and therefore retained some acidity and freshness, after which she uttered the famous words, 'not like all those spoofulated Chardonnays being made in the Valley these days.'"

Eatymology

≡ THE ART OF SPOOFULATION ≡

Spoofulation is in the eye of the beholder, as some of the most railed against wine-making techniques are considered standard by many vintners. These are some of the ways many winemakers adjust wine production or "spoofulate" it, for better or for worse:

Micro-oxygenation: To speed up the aging process.

Enzymes: To remove solids from the juice, enhance aroma, and intensify color.

Oak extracts: To add flavor.

Sugar: To lengthen fermentation and increase alcohol content.

Acid: To increase acidity.

Water: To lower alcohol level.

Yeast: Selected strains added to guide fermentation.

Stabilizers: To lengthen the shelf life of bottles.

≡ ANTONYM ≡

The opposite of spoofulated wines might well be so-called natural wines that eschew any additives. While there is no industry standard for natural wine, wine writer Alice Feiring, an authority on the category, defines them thusly: "It needs to be natural from the ground up. Nothing added, nothing taken away. No additives, no adjustments, and very little added sulfur."

TRIG•GER FOODS (*noun*):

Foods that by their very presence exercise an influence over the selection of other foods.

. . . .

≡ ORIGINS ≡

A 2012 study published in the *Agricultural and Resource Economics Review* by scientists at Cornell University introduced the idea of trigger foods as comestibles that can influence food choices simply through their physical presence. The researchers collected data on how the placement of certain items in school cafeterias affected food choices by students. They found that sweet treats were less popular on days when bananas and green beans were served in the cafeteria line but more popular on days when celery, applesauce, and fruit cocktail were available. For example, the presence of bananas made ice cream 11 to 16 percent less popular, and the presence of fruit cocktail made Little Debbie snacks 7 to 9 percent more popular.

≡ CARROT OR (CELERY) STICK APPROACH ≡

In an earlier study published in 2009 in *Choices*, 120 junior high participants were told they must take carrots with their lunch, while another 120 were given a choice between carrots or celery. Of those required to take the carrots, 69 percent ate them, while 91 percent of students choosing between carrots or celery ate the carrots. Merely the presence of a choice of celery increased carrot consumption by 20 percent. "Such results suggest that requiring a vegetable, while offering an active choice between at least two options substantially reduces the waste from vegetables, and increases the nutritional content of the foods consumed," wrote the study's authors, David R. Just and Brian Wansink.

═ OTHER USES ═

Trigger food has also been used to describe those items that can stimulate overeating or aggravate medical conditions such as irritable bowel syndrome, migraine headaches, gout, and acid reflux, among others.

TWEC·I·PES (*noun*): Extremely abbreviated recipes, published via Twitter, that provide cooking instructions in no more than 140 characters.

≡ ORIGINS ≡

A 2009 article in the *Guardian* noted the new social media trend of highly abbreviated recipes posted by Twitter users, including @twecipe, a Twitter account that promised to reply with instructions for a dish in response to a tweeted list of ingredients.

≡ #GLOSSARY ≡

Some common twecipe abbreviations, according to the Twitter @Cookbook Glossary:

bqtgarni: bouquet garni

btn: beaten

clv: clove

lyr: layer

roma: Roma tomato

sesseed: sesame seeds

t: teaspoon

T: tablespoon

tom: tomato

turm: turmeric powder

whtflr: whole wheat flour

zuke: zucchini

≡ PSTA AL CRDO ≡

Italian chef Giorgio Locatelli's twecipe for pasta al crudo, published in the *Guardian* in 2009: "Mix hndflcapers /blckolvs/bsil/5ancho-vies, 3Tpassata, 5Tolvoil. Season. Pour ovr spag."

≡ TWOOKBOOK ≡

In 2010, Maureen Evans, an early twecipe pioneer (@cookbook), published *Eat Tweet*, the first ever Twitter cookbook featuring 1,020 twecipes. "I do this as a coffee-break hobby," she told the *New York Times* in 2009. "Kind of like sudoku. I really get a kick out of how complex a recipe I can fit into 140 characters."

"It may not be the case, as an editor told me, that Twitter is the first great recipe innovation in 200 years. But it doesn't have to be. Unpacking tweets for an hour or so in the kitchen is surprisingly challenging. It forces the mind to think harder, to fill gaps, to innovate and improvise. It re-introduces risk and discovery to cooking, which puts you only a short distance from delight."

—LAWRENCE DOWNES, JOURNALIST AND TWECIPE CONVERT

UG·LY FRUIT (*noun*):

Imperfect produce once destined for the trash bin but newly popular after outcries about food waste.

≡ ORIGINS ≡

The term refers to blemished or imperfect produce restricted by the European Union as well as by retailers. Critics have complained that the food rules cause as much as 20 to 40 percent of fresh produce in Europe to be wasted. Marketing standards for twenty-six types of produce were finally relaxed by the EU in 2009 but still persist in supermarkets.

≡ BACKLASH ≡

In response to a European Union declaration of 2014 as the Year Against Food Waste, ugly fruit is newly popular in Europe. Intermarché, France's third-largest supermarket chain, launched a campaign for the "grotesque apple," "disfigured eggplant," and other ugly fruits and vegetables, selling them at deep discounts. In Portugal, a food cooperative called Fruta Feia ("Ugly Fruit") buys imperfect fruit from farmers and sells it for low prices. Moreover, UK supermarket Waitrose began selling "weather blemished" apples in its stores.

≡ PERFECT FRUIT ≡

The opposite of ugly fruit can be found at the Tokyo shop Sembikiya, which specializes in selling the most flawless, picture-perfect fruits—displayed like high-end jewelry—as gifts. There, you can find twenty-five-dollar apples, strawberries that fetch eighty-three dollars per dozen, and melons that cost more than one hundred dollars apiece.

"If most Brits had half an idea of the amount going to waste, they'd be snapping up ugly veg by the trolley load. There's no difference in taste or nutritional value. This is perfectly good food that could and should be eaten by humans."

—JAMIE OLIVER, CELEBRITY CHEF

URGE SURF•ING (*noun*):
A technique, based on mindfulness, that involves "riding out" a food urge or craving until it passes without giving in.

....

≡ ORIGINS ≡

Urge surfing was coined by G. Alan Marlatt, PhD, a professor of psychology at the University of Washington. In a 2009 interview, he recounted the origins of the concept: "The idea for urge surfing came from a man who was trying to stop smoking... I explained to him that an urge is like an ocean wave that grows bigger and bigger as it approaches the shore. As it grows, there's the desire to just give in, but if you do, you'll reinforce the power of the addiction. Instead, you can ride the 'wave' by using the breath as a kind of surfboard. It turns out this smoker was also a surfer, and the image of the wave really helped him."

≡ MALT BALL SURFING ≡

In *Dialectical Behavior Therapy for Binge Eating and Bulimia* (2009), authors Debra L. Safer, Christy F. Telch, and Eunice Y. Chen provide the following example of how to urge surf a craving for malt balls: "Take one of the malt balls but do not eat it. Smell it, be aware of any salivation. Be mindful of any thoughts, feelings, or judgments that arise. Be aware of any urges to eat the malt ball... Just urge surf, riding the urge out... At the end of this exercise, get in touch with your Wise Mind to decide whether to eat the malt ball or not. If you choose to eat it, do so as a conscious choice to eat it—and do so mindfully."

≡ SCIENCE ≡

A 2013 study in the *British Journal of Health Psychology* examined the effects of urge surfing and other "acceptance" strategies compared with cognitive defusion, another mindfulness technique, in individuals trying to reduce the amount of chocolate they consumed. The researchers found that those in the cognitive defusion group ate significantly less chocolate over a five-day period and that acceptance techniques, including urge surfing, failed to help individuals resist chocolate.

VEG·E·TA·BLE BUTCH·ER (*noun*): (1) A person who trims, peels, and otherwise prepares fresh vegetables for customers to cook at home. (2) A purveyor of plant-based meat substitutes.

═ CHOP CHOP ═

Mario Batali's Eataly in New York City prominently features a vegetable butcher in its produce department. "If you're not familiar with how to trim an artichoke, we'll trim you an artichoke," Batali told *New York* magazine in 2010. "If you don't think you have time to peel your baby carrots, you can leave them with us and go shop in the other parts of the store, and we'll peel them. We'll do anything but cook them."

═ BLOOD-FREE BUTCHERING ═

De Vegetarische Slager (The Vegetarian Butcher), Europe's first all-vegetarian butcher shop, opened in 2010 in The Hague, offering meat alternatives made from the seeds of the lupine plant, a legume native to the Mediterranean and the Andean highlands of Latin America. Jaap Korteweg, one of the business's owners and an eighth-generation lupine seed farmer, opened the shop to provide a sustainable alternative to meat and products made from soy.

V

═ JACKFRUIT STEAKS ═

With seed money crowdfunded from a 2014 Kickstarter campaign, the brother-sister team of Kale (yes, his name is Kale) and Aubry Walch plan to open the Herbivorous Butcher, America's first vegan butcher shop, in Minneapolis. Their products will include sausages made from pinto beans and steaks made from jackfruit, which the Walches claim provides the faux meat with a veiny, fibrous texture.

VEN·DRI·FI·CA·TION

(*noun*): The process by which an influx of fancy food trucks selling gourmet treats threatens to displace established street vendors and restaurants.

≡ ORIGINS ≡

Writer Katie Robbins coined the term in a 2009 article for *BlackBook*, reporting on rising tensions in New York neighborhoods between long-standing kebab and hot dog vendors and their new competition: social media–savvy entrepreneurs serving up cupcakes, schnitzel sandwiches, and Tahitian vanilla panna cotta (among other treats) from their high-end food trucks. Robbins writes: "In a city accustomed to gentrification, perhaps this new phenomenon could be described as 'vendrification,' with more expensive, higher-tech carts and trucks sweeping in and shaking up the culinary terrain of the streets."

≡ CRACKDOWN ≡

Following complaints from brick-and-mortar restaurants about the intrusion of gourmet food trucks, the Los Angeles Police Department initiated a crackdown in 2009 on mobile food vendors parked along the Miracle Mile stretch of Wilshire Boulevard. Citations were issued to the food trucks for "illegal vending."

V

≡ EMERGENCY MAKEOVER ≡

New York magazine reported in 2012 that food truck vendors had burnished their image in New York City following Hurricane Sandy, going from "scourge" to "savior." "Because they're self-sufficient and run off their own generators, they were able to pop back into business quicker than a lot of brick-and-mortar establishments," David Weber, president of the New York City Food Truck Association (NYCFTA), told the magazine. "That created this opportunity to use the trucks to provide relief in neighborhoods still without power." According to the NYCFTA, in the first month after Sandy, sixty different food trucks at twenty different locations served 350,000 free meals to New Yorkers in need.

VI·NO·THER·A·PY (*noun*):
Spa treatments using wine and wine by-products.

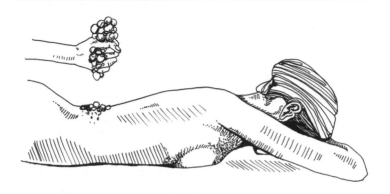

≡ ORIGINS ≡

The French company Caudalie is the preeminent developer of cosmetic and skin care products based on extracts from grape seeds and ingredients from the wine-making process. In 1995, Caudalie registered a patent for extracting and stabilizing grape seed polyphenols, and in 1999, it opened Les Sources de Caudalie, the world's first wine spa, in a castle in the Bordeaux region in France.

≡ WINES BY THE BATH ≡

Kenwood Inn and Spa in Sonoma, California, offers a menu of "wines by the bath," which include a "luxury vinotherapy bath," a glass of wine, and a gift bag of vinotherapy bath products. There's a Pinot Noir Bath, enriched with Red Vine extract, a Chardonnay Bath "comprised of uplifting notes of citrus and grape essential oils mixed with hand-crafted Chardonnay bath salts," and a Sparkling Bath "with sparkling salts as well as enriched grape elixirs."

≡ SPORTS ≡

In 2014, then New York Knicks basketball player Amar'e Stoudemire posted a photo to Instagram of himself soaking in a tub of red wine. "The red wine bath is very important to me because it…creates more circulation in my red blood cells," Stoudemire said. "Plus, it's very hot. So it's like a hot tub. But it's also the red wine just kind of soothes the body."

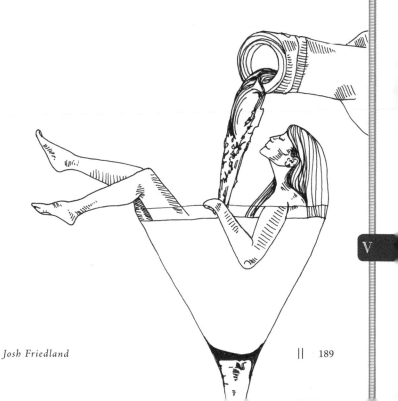

VIR·TU·AL WA·TER

(*noun*): Also known as embedded water, the amount of water that is used in the production of a good or service.

≡ ORIGINS ≡

British geographer John Anthony Allan, PhD, is credited with creating the concept of virtual water in 1993. In his 2011 book *Virtual Water: Tackling the Threat to Our Planet's Most Precious Resource*, Allan explained the idea of virtual water by looking at the amount of water "hidden" in a cup of espresso: "Let's start with coffee. Well, you might say, I like my coffee strong. There's barely any water in there at all. Maybe… But what if I told you that in your tiny espresso there is 140 litres of water. Yes—140 litres. You might think I was slightly deranged. But that is the virtual water hidden in the coffee. That is the amount of water used in growing, producing, packaging, and shipping the beans that make the coffee."

≡ WATER FOOTPRINT ≡

Virtual water is closely linked to the concept of a "water footprint," the total virtual water content of all the goods and services consumed by an individual or by the population of one country.

≡ FOODS, RANKED ≡

A 2003 study estimated the virtual water content of foods in Japan:

FOOD	VIRTUAL WATER (IN CUBIC METERS/TON)
beef	20,700
pork	5,900
poultry	4,500
rice	3,600
eggs	3,200
soybeans	2,500
wheat	2,000
maize	1,900
milk	560

≡ MARKET FORCES ≡

Writing in the *Wall Street Journal* in 2015, Bill Davidow and Michael S. Malone proposed the creation of a market in virtual water to address drought conditions in California. They suggested giving California's water-intensive almond industry—which consumes 1.2 trillion gallons of water per year—the ability to sell some of the real water it would otherwise use at a high price, making it advantageous for farmers to curtail some almond production or plant more water-efficient crops. "The devil is in the details, notably in getting all that water distributed and sold," observed Davidow and Malone. "But if markets and exchanges can be created for everything from carbon emissions to placing kids in schools, surely they can be built to price and sell virtual water."

WALK·AWAYS (*noun*):
Supermarket customers who leave without completing their purchases due to frustration with checkout lines.

··

≡ LOST REVENUE ≡

A 2009 article published on the trade website Retailcustomerexperience.com defined the problem of walk-aways and their impact as lost revenue: "Research suggests that retailers experience an average of 1.6 percent of customers leaves [sic] the checkout queue—and the store—without completing the purchase... They're dropping the items and are walking away. We call them walk-aways."

≡ LINE LINGO ≡

The retail industry and the researchers who study "queue science" have their own unique language for talking about the movement of people though lines:

Balking: When customers decide not to join the line if it is too long.

Faffing: The delay when shoppers gather their things at checkout after completing their purchases.

Jockeying: When customers switch between lines if they think they will check out quicker.

Lane per lane: The typical form of queuing found in grocery stores.

Queue busting: A technique aimed at eliminating lines by giving retail employees mobile platforms to process sales.

Reneging: Leaving a line after spending some time waiting.

Sweethearting: A practice detrimental to the bottom line whereby store employees give away items to loyal customers by not ringing up every item.

Virtual queuing: Typically found in bakeries or delis, where customers don't get into a line but take a number and are called in order.

≡ SMART CARTS ≡

According to a 2015 article in the *Daily Mail*, the design firm Cambridge Consultants has developed a sensor device that fits into the wheels of supermarket carts and transmits data via Bluetooth about shoppers' locations in real time. The technology could help reduce long lines and potentially reduce walkaways by alerting supermarkets when shoppers are nearing checkouts, allowing managers to allocate cashiers when and where they are needed most.

WHITE WHALE (*noun*):

A rare, elusive beer, typically in limited production, that is highly sought after by beer aficionados.

....

═ BEER TRADING ═

White whale is a common term in beer trading circles, where beer lovers come together in online forums to barter for hard-to-find bottles. White whales are considered the rarest, most in demand brews among beer traders.

According to a 2015 blog post on Eater.com, the frenzy over these uncommon beers has generated a bit of controversy in beer circles: "There are many purists who believe that beer should be a drink of the people. It should be accessible, readily available, and preferably local. These drinkers chafe against what they see as the 'wineification' of beer, the idea that beers are being used as commodity focusing on status and price instead of flavor. But, others relish the idea of tasting that rare and delicious white whale. To the hunter, drinking a near extinct beer is exhilarating, and he/she will go to great lengths to find the given beer."

═ DESPERATELY SEEKING SUDS ═

A list of beers published in 2014 on the website Talkbeer .com ranked Cantillon Soleil de Minuit (1999), a cloudberry lambic beer brewed in Sweden, as the most sought after white whale in the world.

≡ BOOK BEER ≡

In 2012, Oregon bookseller Powell's Books teamed up with craft brewer Rogue Ale and Spirits to create White Whale Ale, a beer brewed with pages from a copy of *Moby Dick*.

≡ GHOST WHALES ≡

The most elite and elusive white whales—the rarest of rare beers—are known as *ghost whales* and can fetch more than $4,000 among private collectors. According to *All About Beer*, for a beer to be deemed a ghost whale, "it must not only come from a deeply respected producer, but also have a scarcity that limits remaining bottles to numbers you learned to count to in kindergarten."

W

WINE APART·MENTS

(*noun*): An apartment complex targeted to wine lovers featuring a shared underground wine cellar and wine bar.

≡ ORIGINS ≡

In 2013, the world's first wine apartment complex opened in Tokyo's upscale Shibuya district. The rental complex aimed at oenophiles houses a temperature- and humidity-controlled cellar in the basement for ten thousand bottles, a wine bar and bistro on the first floor, and a private sommelier. Residents also have access to a collection of one hundred different types of wineglasses displayed in the building's lobby.

≡ PERKS ≡

The eighteen apartment units at the complex are furnished with:

+ A glass showcase for displaying wineglasses
+ A white tabletop tasting counter
+ A wine cooler for daily wine storage
+ Floors made of oak, just like wine barrels

≡ WINE RESIDENCE ≡

In 2012, it was reported that quarterback Peyton Manning had moved into the sprawling sixteen-thousand-square-foot former home of Denver Broncos coach Mike Shanahan, which contained a "wine residence." "What's a wine residence?" the website Grapefriend.com pondered. "I have no idea. But I imagine it to be like the most awesome guest house ever, with giant fridges, wines on tap in every room, glasses within a hand's reach, servers to provide you with whatever grapes you're in the mood for at whatever minute of the day."

≡ WINE HOTELS ≡

In 2014, vinotherapy company Caudalie (see page 188) took over the management of the Royal Champagne Hotel, a five-star hotel in the Champillon district between Reims and Epernay. Caudalie declared that the project was the first step in "developing a collection of French wine hotels."

W

WINE RAVE (*noun*): An all-night party where the music and dancing typical of a traditional rave is lubricated by wine and wine cocktails instead of drugs.

≡ ORIGINS ≡

One of the first wine raves took place at the 2008 San Diego Bay Wine & Food Festival. It promised "twenty-five of the edgiest wine and spirits on the market today [to] get things going while wine and foodie fans frolic and dance the night away."

≡ WHAT TO EXPECT ≡

According to a 2015 report on wine raves in the *Los Angeles Times*, the parties typically begin after 11:00 p.m. and last long into the night featuring DJs, dancing, and wine-based cocktails that glow under black light.

≡ MODERN BACCHANALS ≡

The mission statement of Wineravela.com: "Wine rave is a state of mind. Can you free yourself from color: its sensations as pleasure; as life. Stop swirling. Derobe. Become bioilluminescent. Feel a stranger. Listen. Laugh and have fun. Wine rave."

W

"I went in to the Wine Rave thinking I would get some lessons on pairing wine with pharmaceutical-grade molly, but that wasn't the case. The wine was delicious, however, and I also liked that I got to drink plenty of it. A big plus in my book."

—ALISON STEVENSON, WINE RAVE NEOPHYTE

≡ FOOD RAVES ≡

The wine rave phenomenon was preceded by what the *New York Times* dubbed "food raves" in a 2011 article on the popularity of urban night markets serving up live music and trendy bites.

ZIP CODE WIN•ERY

(*noun*): A winery that seeks to associate itself with a wine-making region more desirable than the region where its vineyards are actually located.

═ ORIGINS ═

The earliest citation for zip code wineries can be found in a 2008 VinVillageRadio interview with Stuart Smith, founder of Smith-Madrone Vineyards & Winery. Smith recounted the growth of wine making in the Napa Valley since he first opened Smith-Madrone in 1971 and the arrival of zip code wineries in the following decades: "When I started, I think there were approximately 30 wineries in the Napa Valley. Today, there are close to three or four hundred and another four or five hundred of what I call Zip Code wineries: labels with no winery. They are made somewhere for the proprietor of the label."

═ BIG BUSINESS ═

In a 2009 profile of wine business mogul Fred Franzia in the *New Yorker*, writer Dana Goodyear explained how Franzia's popular Charles Shaw wine (also known as "Two Buck Chuck") gains from the prestige associated with the Napa Valley wine region—where it is bottled—even though it is made from cheaper grapes grown in vineyards in California's less desirable Central Valley: "Although Charles Shaw wine falls under the generic California appellation, the broadest possible designation, it can legitimately be labelled 'Cellared & Bottled by Charles Shaw Winery, Napa, CA,' a practice that strikes many in Napa as unsavory. 'It's called a Zip Code winery,' Vic Motto, a business adviser to Napa Valley wineries, says. 'The unsuspecting consumer may not realize it's not Napa wine. Fred uses that to his advantage.'"

≡ ZIP DECODER ≡

Zip codes of some of the top wine-making districts of Napa Valley:

    94515 (Calistoga)
    94562 (Oakville)
    94573 (Rutherford)
    94574 (St. Helena)
    94599 (Yountville)

Z

SOURCES

INTRODUCTION

Schama, Simon. *Scribble, Scribble, Scribble: Writing on Politics, Ice Cream, Churchill, and My Mother*. New York: Ecco, 2011.

APORKALYPSE

"Carl's Jr. Tests 'Aporkalypse' Breakfast Sandwich." *Brand Eating* (blog). Accessed February 15, 2015. www.brandeating.com/2014/12/carls-jr-tests-aporkalypse-breakfast-sandwich.html.

"FAOSTAT." Food and Agriculture Organization of the United Nations Statistics Division. Accessed February 15, 2015. http://faostat3.fao.org/home/E.

Green, Martin. "Aporkalypse Now as Welsh Brewer Launches Chocolate and Bacon Beer." *Off Licence News*, August 8, 2013. http://offlicencenews.co.uk/news/fullstory.php/aid/13524/Aporkalypse_now_as_Welsh_brewer_launches_chocolate_and_bacon_beer.html.

Hogsback Brewing Company. Accessed February 15, 2015. http://hogsback.ca/.

Leibovich, Mark, and Grant Barrett. "The Buzzwords of 2009." *New York Times*, December 19, 2009. www.nytimes.com/2009/12/20/weekinreview/20buzz.html?_r=2&.

Satran, Joe. "Bacon Shortage 'Aporkalypse' Theoretically Possible, But Highly Unlikely, Given Basic Economics." *Huffington Post*, September 28, 2012. www.huffingtonpost.com/2012/09/28/bacon-shortage_n_1920575.html.

"Sportsman Channel Unleashes a Full Week of 'Aporkalypse 2014.'" PigmanTV.com, July 24, 2014. www.pigmantv.com/news/sportsman-channel-unleashes-a-full-week-of-aporkalypse-2014.

ARUGULANCE

Bates, Michael. "Typical Liberal Arugulance." *BatesLine* (blog). Accessed February 15, 2015. www.batesline.com/archives/2007/08/typical-liberal.html.

Claiborne, Craig. "Food News: A Green by Any Name." *New York Times*, May 24, 1960.

Dowd, Maureen. "The Aura of Arugulance." *New York Times*, April 19, 2009. www.nytimes.com/2009/04/19/opinion/19dowd.html.

"Eruca Sativa." *Wikipedia*. Accessed February 15, 2015. http://en.wikipedia.org/wiki/Eruca_sativa.

Zeleny, Jeff. "Obama's Down on the Farm." *The Caucus* (blog), *New York Times*, July 27, 2007. http://thecaucus.blogs.nytimes.com/2007/07/27/obamas-down-on-the-farm/.

BARISTA WRIST

Bernson, Alex. "Real Talk: Barista Health In The Workplace—Part One." Sprudge, January 7, 2013. http://sprudge.com/real-talk-barista-health-in-the-workplace-part-one.html.

_____. "Real Talk: Barista Health In The Workplace—Part Two." Sprudge, January 9, 2013. http://sprudge.com/real-talk-barista-health-in-the-workplace-part-two.html.

Callahan, Maureen. "Baristas Feeling the Grind with Repetitive Stress Injuries." *New York Post*, May 4, 2014. http://nypost.com/2014/05/04/baristas-feeling-the-grind-with-repetitive-stress-injuries/.

Martineau, Chantal. "Barista Wrist: It's Real!" Food Republic, July 29, 2011. www.foodrepublic.com/2011/07/29/barista-wrist-its-real.

BEER MILE

"Beer Mile World Championships." Flotrack. Accessed February 15, 2015. www.flotrack.org/beermileworlds/#rules.

Crouse, Lindsay. "Cue the 'Chariots of Fire' Theme, With Burps." *New York Times*, December 2, 2014. www.nytimes.com/2014/12/03/sports/cue-the-chariots-of-fire-theme-with-burps.html.

"Frequently Asked Questions." Beermile. Accessed February 15, 2015. www.beermile.com/faq.beer.

Soong, Kelyn. "Beer Mile World Championships Winner Drinks Four Beers and Runs a Mile in Five Minutes." *Washington Post*, December 4, 2014. www.washingtonpost.com/blogs/early-lead/wp/2014/12/04/beer-mile-world-championships-winner-drinks-four-beers-and-runs-a-mile-in-five-minutes/.

Swaby, Rachel. "The Untold History of the Beer Mile." *Runner's World*, September

24, 2014. www.runnersworld.com/races/the-untold-history-of-the-beer
-mile?page=single.

BESTOVORE

Elton, Sarah. "Going Glocal: Ideas from Afar Meet Food from Home." *Globe and Mail*, June 15, 2010. www.theglobeandmail.com/life/going-glocal-ideas
-from-afar-meet-food-from-home/article1373164/.

Gordon, Peter. "Peter Gordon: 'Our Love Affair with Home-Grown Ingredients Is Killing Innovation in Our Restaurants.'" *Independent*, March 11, 2010. www
.independent.co.uk/life-style/food-and-drink/features/peter-gordon
-our-love-affair-with-homegrown-ingredients-is-killing-innovation-in
-our-restaurants-1919364.html.

McWilliams, James E. *Just Food: Where Locavores Get It Wrong and How We Can Truly Eat Responsibly*. New York: Little, Brown and Company, 2009.

"Oxford Word Of The Year: Locavore." *OUPblog*, November 12, 2007. http://blog
.oup.com/2007/11/locavore/.

Stein, Joshua David. "Mimi Sheraton on Bestavores, Brooklyn, and Bygones." Eater. Accessed February 15, 2015. www.eater.com/2011/1/18/6701485
/mimi-sheraton-on-bestavores-brooklyn-and-bygones.

BISTRONOMY

Muhlke, Christine. "Bistronomy." *New York Times*, January 28, 2007. www.nytimes
.com/2007/01/28/magazine/28food.t.html.

Palling, Bruce. "Better, Cheaper French Cuisine." *Wall Street Journal*, September 10, 2010. www.wsj.com/articles/SB10001424052748704644404575482
180005592958.

Samuel, Henry. "Growth of 'Bistronomy' as French Chefs Fall on Hard Times." *Telegraph*, June 20, 2011. www.telegraph.co.uk/news/worldnews/europe/france
/8587950/Growth-of-bistronomy-as-French-chefs-fall-on-hard-times.html.

Sigal, Jane. "Yves Camdeborde: The Paris Chef of the Moment." *Food & Wine*, January 2007. www.foodandwine.com/articles/yves-camdeborde-the
-paris-chef-of-the-moment.

Worthen, Shana. "Bistronomy." *One Peppercorn* (blog), October 4, 2009. http://
onepeppercorn.com/2009/10/bistronomy/.

BLOOD CASHEWS

Amon, Joseph. "National Cashew Day More than Nuts." Human Rights Watch, October 3, 2011. www.hrw.org/news/2011/10/03/national-cashew-day
-more-nuts.

"Anti-Human Trafficking Coalition Launches Campaign to Boycott 'Blood Cashews' from Vietnam." Democratic Voice of Vietnam, June 13, 2012. http://dvov.org/2012/06/13/anti-human-trafficking-coalition-launches -campaign-to-boycott-blood-cashews-from-vietnam/.

Human Rights Watch. *The Rehab Archipelago: Forced Labor and Other Abuses in Drug Detention Centers in Southern Vietnam.* New York: Human Rights Watch, 2011.

Marshall, Andrew. "From Vietnam's Forced-Labor Camps: 'Blood Cashews.'" *Time*, September 6, 2011. http://content.time.com/time/world/article /0,8599,2092004,00.html?iid=pf-main-mostpop1.

BLUEWASHING

"Bluewash." *Wikipedia*. Accessed February 15, 2015. http://en.wikipedia.org /wiki/Bluewash.

Cressey, Daniel. "Fight over Sustainable Seafood Labelling Flares up." *News Blog, Nature*, April 12, 2013. http://blogs.nature.com/news/2013/04/fight -over-sustainable-seafood-labelling-flares-up.html.

Jacquet, Jennifer, et al. "Conserving Wild Fish in a Sea of Market-Based Efforts." *Oryx* 44, no. 01 (January 2010): 45. doi:10.1017/S0030605309990470.

"NGOs Criticize 'Blue Washing' by the Global Compact." Global Policy Forum, July 4, 2007. www.globalpolicy.org/global-taxes/32267-ngos-criticize -qblue-washingq-by-the-global-compact.html.

BONE BROTH

Moskin, Julia. "Bone Broth Evolves From Prehistoric Food to Paleo Drink." *New York Times*, January 6, 2015. www.nytimes.com/2015/01/07/dining /bone-broth-evolves-from-prehistoric-food-to-paleo-drink.html.

Odell, Kat. "200 Broth-Starved New Yorkers Are Lining Up Daily for Marco Canora's Brodo. Why?" Eater NY, December 30, 2014. http://ny.eater .com/2014/12/30/7422679/whats-the-deal-with-brodo-and-why -should-or-shouldnt-you-care.

Pardilla, Caroline. "Would You Drink a Bone Broth Cocktail?" Eater, January 21, 2015. www.eater.com/drinks/2015/1/21/7863997/pistola-debuts -bone-broth-cocktails.

BONE LUGE

Bone Luge. Accessed February 15, 2015. www.boneluge.com/.

Brones, Anna. "Bone Luge: A Food Trend Gone Wrong?" *Huffington Post*, January 31, 2012. www.huffingtonpost.com/anna-brones/bone-luge_b_1244314.html.

Neuschwander, Hanna. "Marrow Minded." *Portland Monthly*, April 27, 2012.

www.portlandmonthlymag.com/eat-and-drink/articles/bone-luge
-cocktail-may-2012.

BRATOPHOBIA

Achatz, Grant. Twitter Post, January 11, 2014. https://twitter.com/Gachatz
/statuses/422172958090489856.

"Chicago Chef's Crying Baby Tweet Stirs Up Controversy." ABC News video.
January 14, 2014. http://abcnews.go.com/GMA/video/chicago-chefs
-crying-baby-tweet-stirs-controversy-21524631.

Krader, Kate. "No Kidding! Children Not Welcome to Dine Here." *Eatocracy* (blog),
CNN, September 20, 2013. http://eatocracy.cnn.com/2013/09/20/no
-kidding-children-not-welcome-to-dine-here/.

"Nippers Not Wanted." *Economist*, June 21, 2014. www.economist.com/news
/united-states/21604597-rights-and-wrongs-banning-babies-nippers
-not-wanted.

Rosario, Frank, and Joe Tacopino. "Brooklyn Pub Bans Kids after Being
Swamped by Families." *New York Post*, May 21, 2014. http://nypost
.com/2014/05/21/brooklyn-pub-bans-kids-after-being-swamped-by
-families/.

BROCAVORE

Hodgman, John. "Brocavore." *Judge John Hodgman* podcast audio. Posted by Julia
Smith July 2, 2014. www.maximumfun.org/judge-john-hodgman/judge
-john-hodgman-episode-167-brocavore.

Jamie. "The Food Diary of a Brocavore." Ann Street Studio, May 12, 2010. http://
annstreetstudio.com/2010/05/12/the-food-diary-of-a-brocavore/.

Muhlke, Christine. "Brocavore." *T Magazine Blog, New York Times*, January 27,
2010. http://tmagazine.blogs.nytimes.com/2010/01/27/word-of-the
-moment-brocavore/.

———. Email Interview, January 15, 2015.

BROCCOLI MANDATE

Dowd, Maureen. "'I'm President,' So No More Broccoli!" *New York Times*, March 23,
1990. www.nytimes.com/1990/03/23/us/i-m-president-so-no-more
-broccoli.html.

Stewart, James B. "How Broccoli Became a Symbol in the Health Care Debate."
New York Times, June 13, 2012. www.nytimes.com/2012/06/14
/business/how-broccoli-became-a-symbol-in-the-health-care-debate.html.

———. "If the Health Care Mandate Goes, the Commerce Clause Might Follow."

New York Times, March 30, 2012. www.nytimes.com/2012/03/31
/business/the-health-care-mandate-and-the-constitution.html.

BROGURT

"Activia." *Wikipedia*. Accessed February 15, 2015. http://en.wikipedia.org/wiki
/Activia.

Bruce, Bill. "Danone for Men Launches in Bulgaria." FoodBev.com, August 2,
2013. www.foodbev.com/news/danone-for-men-launches-in-bulgaria
#.VODlHcaKq2y.

———. "Yogurt for Men: A Slow but Powerful Trend." FoodBev.com, January 7,
2015. www.foodbev.com/opinion/yogurt-for-men-a-slow-but-powerful
-trend#.VODlY8aKq2z.

Merwin, Hugh. "Brogurt, or Greek 'Yogurt for Men,' Is a Real Thing."
Grub Street (blog), *New York*, February 25, 2013. www.grubstreet
.com/2013/02/powerful-yogurt-greek-yogurt-for-men.html.

Powerful Yogurt. Accessed February 15, 2015. www.powerful.yt.

Zuckerman, Esther. "Here Comes 'Brogurt.'" *Wire*, February 25, 2013. www
.theatlanticwire.com/entertainment/2013/02/here-comes-brogurt
/62495/.

BUZZ BARS

Chappell, Bill. "Stoutaccino? Starbucks Tests Coffee With Beer Flavors." *The
Two-Way* (blog), NPR, September 23, 2014. www.npr.org/blogs/thetwo
-way/2014/09/23/350889056/stoutaccino-starbucks-tests-coffee-with
-beer-flavors.

Gallegos, Emma. "Now Serving at Starbucks: Wine, Beer & Small Plates." LAist,
December 19, 2012. http://laist.com/2012/12/19/now_serving_at
_starbucks_wine_beer.php.

Katz, Jon. "10 Coffee Beers That Pull Serious Double-Duty." Food Republic,
August 14, 2013. www.foodrepublic.com/2013/08/14/10-coffee-beers
-pull-serious-double-duty.

Raab, Lauren. "Starbucks Tries Offering Beer-Flavored Dark Barrel Latte." *Los
Angeles Times*, September 23, 2014. www.latimes.com/food/dailydish
/la-dd-starbucks-beer-latte-20140922-story.html.

"Starbucks Evenings." Starbucks. Accessed March 30, 2015. www.starbucks.com
/coffeehouse/starbucks-stores/starbucks-evenings.

Swan, Raygan. "New Buzz Bars Serve Beer and Wine, as Well as Java."
Indianapolis Star, September 11, 2012. http://archive.indystar.com
/article/20120911/OUTTOEAT/209130312/New-buzz-bars-serve
-beer-wine-well-java.

"Tryst Coffeehouse." DCBeer.com. Accessed March 30, 2015. www.dcbeer.com
/venue/tryst-coffeehouse.

CAKE SPLOSHING

Burgess, Martha. "M Burgess: Performing Audience," February 28, 2014. http://
static1.squarespace.com/static/5199cd8de4b0191970591a5e/t/5304f
264e4b0ef33e63027aa/1392833124652/Press+Release+%28website
%29.pdf.

Druckman, Charlotte. "Sit on It." *Paris Review Daily* (blog), April 2, 2014. www
.theparisreview.org/blog/2014/04/02/sit-on-it/.

Jansson, Tove. *Comet in Moominland*. Translated by Elizabeth Portch. New York:
Square Fish, 2010.

Lyle, Sparky. *The Bronx Zoo*. New York: Dell Publishing Co., 1980.

"Wet and Messy Fetishism." *Wikipedia*. Accessed February 15, 2015. http://
en.wikipedia.org/wiki/Wet_and_messy_fetishism.

CARNISM

Beyond Carnism. Accessed February 15, 2015. www.carnism.org/.

"Humane Myth Glossary: Neocarnism." Humane Myth. Accessed February 21,
2015. www.humanemyth.org/glossary/1034.htm.

Joy, Melanie. "Dis-Ease of the Heart: The Psychology of Eating Animals." Forks
Over Knives, May 23, 2012. www.forksoverknives.com/dis-ease-of-the
-heart-the-psychology-of-eating-animals/.

———. *Why We Love Dogs, Eat Pigs, and Wear Cows: An Introduction to Carnism*.
Berkeley, CA; Enfield: Conari Press, 2011.

CARROTMOB

Burkeman, Oliver. "Flash Mobs Face Ban after Pillow Fight Fiasco in San Francisco."
Guardian, March 10, 2009. www.theguardian.com/world/2009/mar/11
/pillow-fight-ban-san-francisco.

Caplan, Jeremy. "Shoppers, Unite! Carrotmobs Are Cooler than Boycotts."
Time, May 15, 2009. http://content.time.com/time/magazine/article
/0,9171,1901467,00.html.

"Carrotmob—Vote with Your Money." Carrotmob. Accessed February 15, 2015.
http://carrotmob.org/.

"Flash Mob." *Wikipedia*. Accessed February 15, 2015. http://en.wikipedia.org
/wiki/Flash_mob.

CAT CAFÉ

"Cat Café." *Wikipedia*. Accessed February 15, 2015. http://en.wikipedia.org/wiki/Cat_caf%C3%A9.

Cha, Frances. "Japan's 'Anti-Loneliness' Cafe Goes Viral." CNN, May 16, 2014. www.cnn.com/2014/05/15/travel/japan-moomin-cafe/index.html.

Ho, Erica. "A Goat Café in Tokyo Wins Over City Dwellers." *Time*, July 13, 2013. http://newsfeed.time.com/2013/07/17/a-goat-cafe-in-tokyo-wins-over-city-dwellers/.

Kulp, Patrick. "The Country's First Cat Cafe Is Here, and It's Just the Beginning." Mashable, November 2, 2014. http://mashable.com/2014/11/03/oakland-cat-cafe/.

Lemmin-Woolfrey, Ulrike. "Cat-Ching! Cat Cafes Take over World." CNN, June 16, 2014. www.cnn.com/2014/06/16/travel/cat-cafes-world/index.html.

Smith, Nicole. "A Trip to Bau House Dog Cafe in Seoul." *Bitten By the Travel Bug* (blog), November 25, 2013. http://bittenbythetravelbug.com/bau-house-dog-cafe-in-seoul/.

CHERPUMPLE

Bake It in a Cake. Accessed February 15, 2015. http://bakeitinacake.com/.

Delahoussaye, James. "The 3-Bird Turducken Has Nothing On This 17-Bird Royal Roast." *The Salt* (blog), NPR, November 21, 2014. www.npr.org/blogs/thesalt/2014/11/21/365509503/the-3-bird-turducken-has-nothing-on-this-17-bird-royal-roast.

Fowler, Geoffrey A. "For Those Who Can't Decide on Dessert, Here's the Dish." *Wall Street Journal*, November 6, 2010. www.wsj.com/articles/SB10001424052702304316404575580630406169718.

Wilmore, Jakeisha. "Three Brothers Bakery's Pumpecapple Piecake Is the Turducken of Desserts." Eater, November 12, 2014. http://houston.eater.com/2014/11/12/7204455/three-brothers-bakerys-pumpecapple-piecake-is-the-turducken-of.

CLUB APPLE

Charles, Dan. "Want To Grow These Apples? You'll Have To Join The Club." *The Salt* (blog), NPR, November 10, 2014. www.npr.org/blogs/thesalt/2014/11/10/358530280/want-to-grow-these-apples-youll-have-to-join-the-club.

Rothman, Lauren. "Club Apples Are the Product of Fruit Dating and Mating." MUNCHIES, November 19, 2014. http://munchies.vice.com/articles/club-apples-are-the-product-of-fruit-dating-and-mating.

"Word Buzz Wednesday: Club Apple, Lumbersexual, Singles Day." *Wordnik* (blog), November 12, 2014. http://blog.wordnik.com/word-buzz -wednesday-club-apple-lumbersexual-singles-day.

COFFEE NAME

"Coffee Aliases Give Cup of 'Joe' New Meaning." *All Things Considered*, NPR, July 28, 2010. www.npr.org/templates/story/story.php?storyId=128828538.

Maggiore, Marina. "Coffee Name." Urban Dictionary, May 9, 2006. www .urbandictionary.com/define.php?term=coffee%20name.

Starbucks Spelling. Accessed February 15, 2015. http://starbucksspelling.tumblr .com/.

COFFEE NAP

Hayashi, Mitsuo, Akiko Masuda, and Tadao Hori. "The Alerting Effects of Caffeine, Bright Light and Face Washing after a Short Daytime Nap." *Clinical Neurophysiology* 114, no. 12 (December 1, 2003): 2268–78. doi:10.1016/S1388-2457(03)00255-4.

Horne, J. A., and L. A. Reyner. "Counteracting Driver Sleepiness: Effects of Napping, Caffeine, and Placebo." *Psychophysiology* 33, no. 3 (May 1996): 306–9.

Howard, Jacqueline. "Yes, Coffee Can Actually Improve The Power Of Your Power Naps." *Huffington Post*, September 3, 2014. www.huffingtonpost .com/2014/09/03/coffee-sleep-power-naps-science_n_5753360.html.

Mann, Jeff. "Caffeine Nap: The Ultimate Power Up." Sleep Junkies, December 5, 2012. http://sleepjunkies.com/tips/the-caffeine-nap/.

Reyner, L. A., and J. A. Horne. "Suppression of Sleepiness in Drivers: Combination of Caffeine with a Short Nap." *Psychophysiology* 34, no. 6 (November 1997): 721–25.

Stromberg, Joseph. "Scientists Agree: Coffee Naps Are Better than Coffee or Naps Alone." Vox, August 28, 2014. www.vox.com/2014/8/28/6074177 /coffee-naps-caffeine-science.

COOKIVORES

Adler, Jerry. "Why Fire Makes Us Human." *Smithsonian Magazine*, June 2013. www.smithsonianmag.com/science-nature/why-fire-makes-us-human -72989884/.

Gorman, Rachael Moeller. "Cooking Up Bigger Brains." *Scientific American*, December 16, 2007. www.scientificamerican.com/article/cooking-up -bigger-brains/.

Lambert, Craig. "The Way We Eat Now." *Harvard Magazine*, June 2004. http://harvardmagazine.com/2004/05/the-way-we-eat-now.html.

Shaw, Jonathan. "Evolution by Fire." *Harvard Magazine*, December 2009. http://harvardmagazine.com/2009/11/cooking-and-human-evolution.

COWPOOLING

Knoblauch, Jessica A. "Cowpooling, or How to Save Money by Buying 700 Pounds of Meat with Your Friends." Mother Nature Network, September 18, 2009. www.mnn.com/your-home/organic-farming-gardening/stories/cowpooling-or-how-to-save-money-by-buying-700-pounds-of-.

Severson, Kim. "A Locally Grown Diet With Fuss but No Muss." *New York Times*, July 22, 2008. www.nytimes.com/2008/07/22/dining/22local.html.

"Yield on Beef Carcass—The Cuts of Beef and Their Average Weights on Whole, Sides and Hind and Front Quarters of Beef." Ask the Meatman. Accessed February 15, 2015. www.askthemeatman.com/yield_on_beef_carcass.htm.

CRINCHY

Hills, Sarah. "New Crisp and Crunch Snack Textures for Value Added Products." FoodNavigator.com, July 2, 2008. www.foodnavigator.com/Market-Trends/New-crisp-and-crunch-snack-textures-for-value-added-products.

"Not Crunchy or Crispy but 'crinchy.'" Ingredion. Accessed February 15, 2015. www.foodinnovation.com/foodinnovation/en-us/RegForms/Documents/Ingredion-Potato_Crisps_Success_Story.pdf.

"TEXICON Food Texture Language Translates Consumer Texture Experience to Speed Product Development." National Starch Food Innovation, September 20, 2011. www.foodinnovation.com/Downloads/Texicon%2020%20September%202011%20Press%20Release.pdf.

CRONUT

"Chef Alina Eisenhauer's 'Dosants' Were Cronuts Before Cronuts Were Cronuts." *Fox News Magazine*, October 18, 2013. http://magazine.foxnews.com/food-wellness/chef-alina-eisenhauers-dosants-were-cronuts-cronuts-were-cronuts.

"Cronut 101." Dominique Ansel Bakery. Accessed February 15, 2015. http://dominiqueansel.com/cronut-101/.

Dixler, Hillary. "Cronuts Are Officially Trademarked Now." Eater, January 15, 2014. www.eater.com/2014/1/15/6296511/cronuts-are-officially-trademarked-now.

Ho, Erica. "Baker Cracks Down on 'Cronut Scalpers.'" *Time*, June 19, 2013.

http://newsfeed.time.com/2013/06/19/baker-cracks-down-on-cronut-scalpers/.

Tidhar, Lily. "The Great Wheel Of Food Mashups." *Co.Design* (blog), September 3, 2014. www.fastcodesign.com/3031349/exclusive-infographic-the-great-wheel-of-food-mashups.

Trowbridge, Denise. "Hilliard Bakery Fights for Trademark on Doughnut-Croissant Hybrid." *Columbus Dispatch*, August 27, 2013. www.dispatch.com/content/stories/business/2013/08/27/battle-for-pastry.html.

"The 25 Best Inventions of the Year 2013." *Time*, November 13, 2013. http://techland.time.com/2013/11/14/the-25-best-inventions-of-the-year-2013/slide/the-cronut/.

CROP MOB

Crop Mob. Accessed February 18, 2015. http://cropmob.org/.

Muhlke, Christine. "Field Report: Plow Shares." *New York Times*, February 28, 2010. www.nytimes.com/2010/02/28/magazine/28food-t-000.html.

Palmer, Kim. "'Crops Mobs' Thrive in Farmville." *StarTribune*, June 23, 2010. www.startribune.com/lifestyle/homegarden/97033299.html.

"Tutorials/Mob Farm." Minecraft Wiki. Accessed February 18, 2015. http://minecraft.gamepedia.com/Tutorials/Mob_farm.

CROP SWAP

Batten, Yvette. "Seeds Planted for Crop-Swap Success." *Taranaki Daily News Online*, September 16, 2013. www.stuff.co.nz/taranaki-daily-news/news/midweek/9171221/Seeds-planted-for-crop-swap-success.

Bickman, Jed. "Losing the War on Poppies." Salon, October 24, 2012. www.salon.com/2012/10/24/losing_the_war_on_poppies/.

Brown, Patricia Leigh. "Urban Farmers Trade Goods and Stories at 'Crop Swaps.'" *New York Times*, November 27, 2014. www.nytimes.com/2014/11/28/us/urban-farmers-trade-goods-and-stories-at-crop-swaps.html.

Finz, Stacy. "Popularity of Crop Swaps Is Growing." *San Francisco Chronicle*, September 4, 2011. www.sfgate.com/food/article/Popularity-of-crop-swaps-is-growing-2310840.php.

Foodswapnetwork.com. Accessed February 21, 2015. http://foodswapnetwork.com/.

Henry, Sarah. "Growing Demand: Crop Swaps Gaining Ground." Shareable, September 27, 2011. www.shareable.net/blog/growing-demand-crop-swaps-gaining-ground.

"Seed Swap." *Wikipedia*. Accessed March 10, 2015. http://en.wikipedia.org/w/index.php?title=Seed_swap&oldid=650795884.

Vann, Cinamon. "Local Crop Swaps Offer More than Fresh Vegetables." *Sacramento Press*, April 3, 2009. http://sacramentopress.com/2009/04/03/local-crop-swaps-offer-more-than-fresh-vegetables/.

DEMITARIAN

"The Barsac Declaration: Environmental Sustainability and the Demitarian Diet." Nitrogen in Europe—European Science Foundation. Accessed February 18, 2015. www.nine-esf.org/Barsac-text.

Harvey, Fiona. "Halve Meat Consumption, Scientists Urge Rich World." *Guardian*, February 17, 2013. www.theguardian.com/environment/2013/feb/18/halve-meat-consumption-scientists.

Vaughan, Adam. "Halving Meat and Dairy Consumption Could Slash Farming Emissions." *Guardian*, April 25, 2014. www.theguardian.com/environment/2014/apr/25/halve-meat-dairy-consumption-slash-emissions-farming.

DRUNKOREXIA

Burke, Sloane C., Jennifer Cremeens, Karen Vail-Smith, and Conrad Woolsey. "Drunkorexia: Calorie Restriction prior to Alcohol Consumption among College Freshman." *Journal of Alcohol and Drug Education* 54, no. 2 (August 2010): 17–34.

Gardner, Jasmine. "My Life as a Drunkorexic." *London Evening Standard*, December 14, 2011. www.standard.co.uk/lifestyle/health/my-life-as-a-drunkorexic-6378543.html.

Kershaw, Sarah. "Starving Themselves, Cocktail in Hand." *New York Times*, March 2, 2008. www.nytimes.com/2008/03/02/fashion/02drunk.html.

Knight, Alissa, and Susan Simpson. "Drunkorexia: An Empirical Investigation of Disordered Eating in Direct Response to Saving Calories for Alcohol Use amongst Australian Female University Students." *Journal of Eating Disorders* 2013, no. 1 (Suppl. 1): P6. Accessed February 18, 2015. www.biomedcentral.com/content/pdf/2050-2974-1-S1-P6.pdf.

DUCKEASY

"Chicago City Council Overturns Foie Gras Ban." Fox News, May 14, 2008. www.foxnews.com/story/2008/05/14/chicago-city-council-overturns-foie-gras-ban.

Gnall, Johnny. "The Birth of the 'Duckeasy.'" *Tasty Morsels* (blog), July 18, 2012. http://johnnygnall.blogspot.com/2012/07/the-birth-of-duckeasy.html.

Hill, Adriene. "Chicago Restaurants Duck a Foie Gras Ban." *All Things*

Considered, NPR, August 22, 2007. www.npr.org/templates/story/story
.php?storyId=13872710.

Parsons, Russ. "Foie Gras Can Go Back on California Menus, Judge Rules." *Los Angeles Times*, January 17, 2015. www.latimes.com/food/dailydish/la-dd
-foie-gras-can-go-back-on-the-menu-judge-rules-20150107-story.html.

Patel, Atish. "India Bans Import of Controversial Foie Gras." *India Real Time* (blog), *Wall Street Journal*, July 7, 2014. http://blogs.wsj.com/india realtime/2014/07/07/india-bans-import-of-controversial-foie-gras/.

Vekshin, Alison, and James Nash. "Foie Gras Goes Underground at California 'Duckeasies.'" *Bloomberg Business*, July 17, 2009. www.bloomberg.com/news
/articles/2012-07-17/foie-gras-goes-underground-at-california-duckeasies-.

EGOTARIAN CUISINE

Rayner, Jay. "Blanchette: Restaurant Review." *Guardian*, April 20, 2014. www
.theguardian.com/lifeandstyle/2014/apr/20/blanchette-restaurant
-review-jay-rayner.

Richman, Alan. "Alan Richman: The Rise of Egotarian Cuisine." *GQ*, March 25, 2014. www.gq.com/life/food/201403/alan-richman-egotarian-cuisine.

FARM GALS

"Entrepreneur Checks on 'Shibuya Gal' Rice Farm." *Japan Times*, August 20, 2009. www.japantimes.co.jp/news/2009/08/20/national/entrepreneur
-checks-on-shibuya-gal-rice-farm/.

Iizumi, Ayako. "Fashionista Farm Gals of Tokyo." *Our World*, January 20, 2010. http://ourworld.unu.edu/en/fashionista-farm-gals-of-tokyo.

Imsomboon, Panicha. "Farm. Food. Hello Kitty." *Modern Farmer*, January 7, 2015. http://modernfarmer.com/2015/01/farm-food-hello-kitty/.

"Japan City Girls Hit Rice Paddies—in Style." *Independent*, December 13, 2009. www.independent.co.uk/life-style/fashion/news/japan-city-girls-hit
-rice-paddies--in-style-1839936.html.

FAST-FOOD ZONING

McDonnell, Patrick J. "Council Limits New Fast-Food Outlets in South L.A." *L.A. Now* (blog), *Los Angeles Times*, December 8, 2010. http://latimesblogs
.latimes.com/lanow/2010/12/council-limits-new-fast-food-outlests-in
-south-los-angeles.html.

Medina, Jennifer. "New Fast-Food Restaurants Are Banned From South L.A." *New York Times*, January 15, 2011. www.nytimes.com/2011/01/16
/us/16fastfood.html.

"No Evidence That Los Angeles Fast-Food Curbs Have Improved Diets or Cut Obesity." RAND Corporation, March 19, 2015. www.rand.org/news /press/2015/03/19.html.

Sturm, Roland, and Deborah A. Cohen. "Zoning For Health? The Year-Old Ban On New Fast-Food Restaurants In South LA." *Health Affairs* 28, no. 6 (December 2009): w1088–97. doi:10.1377/hlthaff.28.6.w1088.

Tsui, Emma. "Reducing Fast Food Outlets through Zoning." Corporations and Health Watch, September 1, 2010. http://corporationsandhealth. org/2010/09/01/reducing-fast-food-outlets-through-zoning/.

"Zoning to Encourage Healthy Eating." Centers for Disease Control and Prevention. Accessed February 18, 2015. www.cdc.gov/phlp/winnable /zoning_obesity.html.

FAT WASHING

Difford, Simon. "Fat-Washing." Difford's Guide, March 27, 2014. www.diffords guide.com/encyclopedia/2014-03-27/328/cocktails/fat-washing.

English, Camper. "The Rise of Olive Oil, Fat, and Butter (!) in Cocktails." *Daily Details* (blog), *Details*, September 26, 2014. www.details.com/blogs /daily-details/2014/09/oil-fat-in-cocktails.html.

Fauchald, Nick. "Secrets of a Cocktail Master." *Food & Wine*, December 2007. www.foodandwine.com/articles/secrets-of-a-cocktail-master.

Laden, Tanja M. "Meat in a Glass: The Carnivore Cocktail." *LA Weekly*, September 23, 2010. www.laweekly.com/restaurants/meat-in-a-glass-the-carnivore -cocktail-2381911.

Liu, Kevin. "The Science of Fat-Washing Cocktails." *Serious Eats*, April 16, 2014. http://drinks.seriouseats.com/2014/04/science-fat-washing-spirits -cocktails-how-fatwashing-works.html.

FELFIE

Axelson, Ben. "What Is a #felfie? Farmers Take Over Social Media with New Trend." Syracuse.com, January 11, 2014. www.syracuse.com/news/index .ssf/2014/01/what_is_a_felfie_farmers_take_over_social_media _with_new_trend.html.

Butcher, Ellis. "'Felfie' Craze Proves a Hit Down on the Cumbrian Farms." *Westmorland Gazette*, January 23, 2014. www.thewestmorlandgazette. co.uk/news/10954661._Felfie__craze_proves_a_hit_down_on_the _Cumbrian_farms/.

"CenturyPly Extends 'khushiyon Ka Rangmanch' with 'felfie Festival.'" Best Media Info, October 1, 2014. www.bestmediainfo.com/2014/10/centuryply -extends-khushiyon-ka-rangmanch-with-felfie-festival/.

"Farmers Journal Facebook Photo Competition Sparks Viral 'Felfie' Trend."
  Irish Farmers Journal, January 2, 2014. www.farmersjournal.ie/farmers
  -journal-facebook-photo-competition-sparks-viral-felfie-trend-153224/.
Felfies. Accessed February 18, 2015. www.felfies.com.
"Finalists in Our 'Selfie on the Farm' Competition." Facebook. Accessed February
  18, 2015. www.facebook.com/media/set/?set=a.10152441514903835.1
  073741843.208480693834&type=1.

FLATBREAD FACTOR

Goh, Brenda. "Bread Was around 30,000 Years Ago: Study." Reuters, October
  18, 2010. www.reuters.com/article/2010/10/18/us-science-bread
  -idUSTRE69H4FT20101018.
GRUMA. Accessed February 18, 2015. www.gruma-en.com/.
Martinez, Alonso, and Ronald Haddock. "The Flatbread Factor."
  Strategy+business, February 28, 2007. www.strategy-business.com/article
  /07106?gko=f499e.
Moroney, Robin. "Every Country Has Its Flatbread Phase." *Informed Reader*
  (blog), *Wall Street Journal*, March 11, 2007. http://blogs.wsj.com
  /informedreader/2007/03/11/every-country-has-its-flatbread-phase/.

FLYING WINEMAKERS

Asimov, Eric. "Satan or Savior: Setting the Grape Standard." *New York Times*,
  October 11, 2006. www.nytimes.com/2006/10/11/dining/11pour.html.
The Flying Winemaker. Accessed February 18, 2015. www.flyingwinemaker.asia/.
"Globalization of Wine." *Wikipedia*. Accessed January 10, 2015. http://en.wikipedia
  .org/w/index.php?title=Globalization_of_wine&oldid=641936927.
Heimoff, Steve. "On 'flying Winemakers': Are They Good or Bad for Wine?"
  Steve Heimoff (blog), May 2, 2014. www.steveheimoff.com/index
  .php/2014/05/02/on-flying-winemakers-are-they-good-or-bad-for
  -wine/.
Janssen, Cory. "Who Are the Flying Winemakers?" WineFrog. Accessed February
  18, 2015. www.winefrog.com/definition/100/flying-winemakers.
Siddle, Richard. "Michel Rolland Defends His Ability to Manage Wines on up to
  200 Wineries around the World." *Harpers Wine & Spirit*, May 1, 2014.
  www.harpers.co.uk/news/michel-rolland-defends-his-ability-to-manage
  -wines-on-up-to-200-wineries-around-the-world/356950.article.
Suckling, James. "Top Gun: Consulting Enologist Michel Rolland Makes Some
  of the World's Best Red Wines." *Wine Spectator*, June 30, 2006. www
  .winespectator.com/wssaccess/show/id/41443.
Veseth, Mike. "Flying Winemakers and the Glocalization of Wine." *Wine Economist*

(blog), July 20, 2008. http://wineeconomist.com/2008/07/20/flying
-winemakers-and-the-glocalization-of-wine/.

FOOD BUBBLE

Brown, Lester R. "India's Dangerous 'Food Bubble.'" *Los Angeles Times*, November
29, 2013. http://articles.latimes.com/2013/nov/29/opinion/la-oe
-brown-india-food-bubble-famine-20131129.

_____. "Lester Brown on Peak Water." *North Denver News*, March 14, 2015.
http://northdenvernews.com/lester-brown-on-peak-water/.

_____. *Plan B: Rescuing a Planet Under Stress and a Civilization in Trouble*. New
York: W. W. Norton & Company, 2003.

Ho, Mae-Wan. "The Food Bubble Economy." Institute of Science in Society,
October 1, 2005. www.i-sis.org.uk/TFBE.php.

Kaufman, Frederick. "The Food Bubble." *Harper's Magazine*, July 2010. http://
harpers.org/archive/2010/07/the-food-bubble/.

FOODING

Caplan-Bricker, Nora. "Dogfooding: Tech Slang for Working out the Glitches."
New Republic, October 28, 2013. www.newrepublic.com/article/115349
/dogfooding-tech-slang-working-out-glitches.

"Fooding." *Wikipedia*. Accessed November 3, 2014. http://en.wikipedia.org/w
/index.php?title=Fooding&oldid=632300029.

Gopnik, Adam. "No Rules!" *New Yorker*, March 29, 2010. www.newyorker.com
/magazine/2010/04/05/no-rules-2.

Lefooding.com. http://lefooding.com/.

FOODIOT

Foodiot KK. Accessed February 18, 2015. www.foodiotkk.com/.

Lempert, Phil. "Welcome 'Koodies'!" Supermarket Guru, November 16, 2009.
www.supermarketguru.com/articles/welcome-%E2%80%9Ckoodies
%E2%80%9D!.html.

Pompeo, Joe. "The Foodiots." *New York Observer*, September 22, 2009. http://
observer.com/2009/09/the-foodiots/.

FOODOIR

"Foodoir." Word Spy, December 15, 2009. http://wordspy.com/index.php
?word=foodoir.

Maxwell, Kerry. "Foodoir." *Macmillan Dictionary Online*, February 24, 2010. www
.macmillandictionary.com/us/buzzword/entries/foodoir.html.

Muhlke, Christine. "Heartburn." *New York Times*, May 29, 2009. www.nytimes
.com/2009/05/31/books/review/Muhlke-t.html.

———. "Kiss the Cook." *New York Times*, December 3, 2009. www.nytimes
.com/2009/12/06/books/review/Muhlke-t.html.

FOOD RACISM

Navarette, Ruben, Jr. "Take Talk of Food Racism with Grain of Salt." CNN,
October 30, 2009. www.cnn.com/2009/OPINION/10/30/navarette
.food.racism/.

Scotting, Andrea. "Diary of a 'Food Racist.'" *Atlantic*, April 14, 2010. www
.theatlantic.com/health/archive/2010/04/diary-of-a-food-racist
/38882/.

Shapiro, Dan. "Eating These Foods Might Make You Racist." MUNCHIES, July
4, 2014. http://munchies.vice.com/articles/eating-these-foods-might
-make-you-racist.

Squires, Nick. "'Discriminatory' Food Names Should Be Banned, Says Austria."
Telegraph, March 9, 2012. www.telegraph.co.uk/news/newstopics
/howaboutthat/9133115/Discriminatory-food-names-should-be
-banned-says-Austria.html.

Vansintjan, Aaron. "The Racism in Healthy Food." *McGill Daily*, October 17,
2013. www.mcgilldaily.com/2013/10/the-racism-in-healthy-food/.

FOOD SWAMP

"Creating Access to Healthy, Affordable Food." USDA Agricultural Marketing
Service. Accessed February 18, 2015. http://apps.ams.usda.gov
/fooddeserts/fooddeserts.aspx.

Maggio, Elizabeth. "South Los Angeles Ban on Fast-Food Chains Misses the
Mark." RAND Corporation, 2009. www.rand.org/pubs/research_briefs
/RB9489/index1.html.

Rose, Donald, J. Nicholas Bodor, Chris M. Swalm, Janet C. Rice, Thomas A.
Farley, and Paul L. Hutchinson. "Deserts in New Orleans? Illustrations of
Urban Food Access and Implications for Policy." University of Michigan
National Poverty Center/USDA Economic Research Service, February
2009. http://npc.fordschool.umich.edu/news/events/food-access/rose
_et_al.pdf.

Sullivan, Daniel Monroe. "From Food Desert to Food Mirage: Race, Social Class,
and Food Shopping in a Gentrifying Neighborhood." *Advances in Applied
Sociology* 4, no. 1 (2014): 30–35. doi:10.4236/aasoci.2014.41006.

FOOD VOICE

Counihan, Carol. "Mexicanas' Food Voice and Differential Consciousness in the San Luis Valley of Colorado." In *Food And Culture: A Reader*, edited by Carol Counihan and Penny Van Esterik, 354–68. New York: Routledge, 2007.

Hauck-Lawson, Annie. "Hearing the Food Voice: An Epiphany for a Researcher." *Digest* 12, no. 1 and 2 (1991).

Hauck-Lawson, Annie, and Jonathan Deutsch. *Gastropolis: Food and New York City*. New York: Columbia University Press, 2010.

GASTRO-ANOMY

Fischler, Claude. "Food Habits, Social Change and the Nature/Culture Dilemma." *Social Science Information* 19, no. 6 (December 1, 1980): 937–53. doi:10.1177/053901848001900603.

McLemee, Scott. "Food Fright." Inside Higher Ed, April 18, 2012. www .insidehighered.com/views/2012/04/18/essay-fear-food-harvey -levenstein.

Schneider, Tanja, and Teresa Davis. "Advertising Food in Australia. Between Antinomies and Gastro-Anomy." *Consumption Markets & Culture* 13, no. 1 (March 2010): 31–41.

GASTROSEXUAL

The Gastrosexual Man. Euromaxx, 2014. www.dw.de/the-gastrosexual-man/av -17931797.

"Gastrosexual of the Month: Winners." The Splendid Table. Accessed March 26, 2015. https://web.archive.org/web/20110623093531/http:// splendidtable.publicradio.org/specials/gastrosexuals/winners.shtml.

Glover, Eleanor. "Rise of the 'Gastrosexual' as Men Take up Cooking in a Bid to Seduce Women." *Daily Mail*, July 21, 2008. www.dailymail.co.uk/femail /article-1036921/Rise-gastrosexual-men-cooking-bid-seduce-women .html.

"Move over Ladies, There's a Gastrosexual in the Kitchen." *Columbus Ledger Enquirer*, April 24, 2013. www.ledger-enquirer.com/2013/04/24/2477157/move -over-ladies-theres-a-gastrosexual.html.

Regan, Tim. "Rant: Is 'Gastrosexual' a Thing?" *Northern Virginia Magazine*, April 9, 2013. www.northernvirginiamag.com/gut-check/2013/04/09/rant -is-gastrosexual-a-thing/.

GOODFELLAS THIN

Carmellini, Andrew, and Gwen Hyman. *Urban Italian: Simple Recipes and True Stories from a Life in Food*. New York: Bloomsbury USA, 2008.

Goodfellas. Directed by Martin Scorsese, 1990.

Hill, Henry, Priscilla Davis, and Nicholas Pileggi. *The Wise Guy Cookbook: My Favorite Recipes From My Life as a Goodfella to Cooking on the Run*. New York: NAL, 2002.

Pileggi, Nicholas. *Wiseguy*. New York: Pocket Books, 2010.

GREASE BANDIT

Colapinto, John. "Hot Grease." *New Yorker*, November 18, 2013. www.newyorker.com/magazine/2013/11/18/hot-grease.

Hundley, Wendy. "Grease Bandits Making a Haul on Used Cooking Oil." *Dallas Morning News*, June 3, 2014. www.dallasnews.com/news/crime/headlines/20140602-grease-bandits-making-a-haul-on-used-cooking-oil.ece.

Hutton, David. "Grease Bandits Take off with 'Liquid Gold.'" *Globe and Mail*, August 1, 2008. www.theglobeandmail.com/news/national/grease-bandits-take-off-with-liquid-gold/article4183953/.

"Lard of the Dance." *Wikipedia*. Accessed December 29, 2014. http://en.wikipedia.org/w/index.php?title=Lard_of_the_Dance&oldid=640060555.

Saulny, Susan. "As Oil Prices Soar, Restaurant Grease Theft Rises." *New York Times*, May 30, 2008. www.nytimes.com/2008/05/30/world/americas/30iht-30grease.13354946.html?pagewanted=all&_r=0.

Wolfe, Wes. "Yellow Grease Thefts Prompt New Law." *Kinston*, January 6, 2013. www.kinston.com/news/local/yellow-grease-thefts-prompt-new-law-1.75011.

GREASE-LOADING

"Crab Rangoon—A Regional Thing?" Chow, February 10, 2003. http://chowhound.chow.com/topics/291841.

Reynolds, Gretchen. "Should Athletes Eat Fat or Carbs?" *Well* (blog), *New York Times*, February 25, 2015. http://well.blogs.nytimes.com/2015/02/25/should-athletes-eat-fat-or-carbs/.

Volek, Jeff S., Timothy Noakes, and Stephen D. Phinney. "Rethinking Fat as a Fuel for Endurance Exercise." *European Journal of Sport Science* 15, no. 1 (January 2, 2015): 13–20. doi:10.1080/17461391.2014.959564.

Wong, Jocelyn. "Coach Said I Could Have Waffle House." *Jocelyn Wong's Blog*, November 7, 2009. http://blogs.teamtbb.com/jocelynwong/2009/11/07/waffle-house/.

GROWLETTE

Friedman, Nancy. "Word of the Week: Growlette." *Fritinancy* (blog), January 12, 2015. http://nancyfriedman.typepad.com/away_with_words/2015/01 /word-of-the-week-growlette.html.

"Growlers Are Gone, Growlettes & Bottles Are Coming!" Throwback Brewery, August 22, 2011. http://throwbackbrewery.com/growlersgone/.

Kidden, Jess. "The History of The Beer Growler." Bottless.net. Accessed February 18, 2015. www.bottless.net/The_History_of_The_Beer _Growler_s/605.htm.

Morgan, Jason. "Growlette: The 32-Ounce Growler." Craft Brewing Business, July 12, 2013. www.craftbrewingbusiness.com/packaging-distribution /growlette-32-ounce-growler-craft-beer/.

HAUTE BARNYARD

"Fancy Free: Model Chad White Has Love For Sail." *Out*, January 30, 2015. www .out.com/fashion/2015/1/30/fancy-free-model-chad-white-has-love-sail.

"Parsing Coffee Buzzwords." Sprudge, April 2, 2014. http://sprudge.com/parsing -coffee-buzzwords-54571.html.

Platt, Adam. "Tasty: The Much-Loved Tasting Room Debuts a New, Larger Space." *New York*, October 2, 2006. http://nymag.com/restaurants /reviews/21649.

_____. "The Haute Barnyard Hall of Fame." *Grub Street* (blog), *New York*, September 26, 2006. www.grubstreet.com/2006/09/the _haute_barnyard_hall_of_fam.html.

HONEY LAUNDERING

Berfield, Susan. "The Honey Launderers: Uncovering the Largest Food Fraud in U.S. History." *Bloomberg View*, September 19, 2013. www.bloomberg .com/bw/articles/2013-09-19/how-germany-s-alw-got-busted-for-the -largest-food-fraud-in-u-dot-s-dot-history#p4.

Elsworth, Catherine. "US Officials Crack down on Chinese 'Honey Laundering.'" *Telegraph*, December 31, 2008. www.telegraph.co.uk/news/worldnews /northamerica/usa/4043733/US-officials-crack-down-on-Chinese -honey-laundering.html.

Lam, Bourree. "The Honey Lobby Is Demanding That the Government Define Honey." *Atlantic*, October 2, 2014. www.theatlantic.com/business /archive/2014/10/the-honey-lobby-is-demanding-that-the-government -defines-honey/380994/.

Smith, Peter Andrey. "A Lab Is Trying to Keep China From Dodging U.S. Tariffs on Honey." *New York Times*, January 19, 2015. www.nytimes

.com/2015/01/20/science/a-lab-is-trying-to-keep-china-from-dodging
-us-tariffs-on-honey.html.

HYPERCOOKING

"First Spin-off Title of 'Senran Kagura' Series! Behold 'Sexy Hyper Cooking
Battle' Competition of 22 Girls! Release of PS Vita Card Version
'Dekamori Senran Kagura' Confirmed for 26 January, 2015!!" PlayStation
.com (Asia), January 23, 2015. https://asia.playstation.com/hk/en
/newsdetail?id=3572.

Newgent, Jackie. *The Big Green Cookbook*. Hoboken, NJ: Houghton Mifflin
Harcourt, 2009.

"Senran Kagura." *Wikipedia*. Accessed March 12, 2015. http://en.wikipedia
.org/w/index.php?title=Senran_Kagura&oldid=650976972.

HYPERPALATABLE

Dvorsky, George. "How 'Hyperpalatable' Foods Could Turn You Into A Food
Addict." *io9*, May 12, 2014. http://io9.com/how-hyperpalatable-foods
-could-turn-you-into-a-food-add-1575144399.

Gearhardt, Ashley N., Carlos M. Grilo, Ralph J. DiLeone, Kelly D. Brownell, and
Marc N. Potenza. "Can Food Be Addictive? Public Health and Policy
Implications." *Addiction* 106, no. 7 (July 2011): 1208–12. doi:10.1111
/j.1360-0443.2010.03301.x.

Kessler, David. *The End of Overeating: Taking Control of Our Insatiable Appetite*.
New York: Penguin Books Limited, 2010.

Moss, Michael. "The Extraordinary Science of Addictive Junk Food." *New York
Times*, February 20, 2013. www.nytimes.com/2013/02/24/magazine
/the-extraordinary-science-of-junk-food.html.

Parker-Pope, Tara. "How the Food Makers Captured Our Brains." *New York Times*,
June 22, 2009. www.nytimes.com/2009/06/23/health/23well.html.

Verner, Amy. "Oreos More Addictive than Cocaine, Study Finds." *The Hot Button
Blog, Globe and Mail*, October 16, 2013. www.theglobeandmail.com
/life/the-hot-button/oreos-more-addictive-than-cocaine-study-finds
/article14885780/.

ICE CHEF

Ellwood, Mark. "Tokyo's Hidden Cocktail Bars." *Departures*, March 20, 2010.
www.departures.com/travel/black-book/tokyo%E2%80%99s-hidden
-cocktail-bars.

"Frederic Tudor." *Wikipedia*. Accessed February 18, 2015. http://en.wikipedia
.org/w/index.php?title=Frederic_Tudor&oldid=647717943.

Korn, Nick. Email Interview, January 27, 2015.

Newman, Kara. "Chiller Theater." *Food Arts*, August 2011. www.foodarts.com /drinks/bar-cellar/13503/chiller-theater.

JANOPAUSE

Adams, Stephen. "Gulp! 'Janopause' Really DOES Work… Giving up Alcohol for a Month Makes You Thinner, Fitter and Helps You Sleep." *Daily Mail*, January 4, 2014. www.dailymail.co.uk/health/article-2533807 /Janopause-really-DOES-work-giving-alcohol-month-makes-thinner -fitter-helps-sleep.html.

"Dry January." *Wikipedia*. Accessed January 22, 2015. http://en.wikipedia.org/w /index.php?title=Dry_January&oldid=643711630.

"Futile to Abstain from Alcohol for a Month." *Times of India*, January 3, 2012. http://timesofindia.indiatimes.com/life-style/health-fitness/health /Futile-to-abstain-from-alcohol-for-a-month/articleshow/11338037 .cms.

"Janopause! It's Worse Than the Menopause—a Month without Alcohol—but Now, at Last, It's Over." *Daily Mail*, January 31, 2002. www.highbeam .com/doc/1G1-82359055.html.

KOKUMI

"Kokumi Experience Report by Dr. Harold McGee." UMAMI Information Center, November 25, 2012. www.umamiinfo.com/2013/01/kokumi -experience-report-by-dr-harold-mcgee-1.php.

"Komi Powder—7400." Nikken. Accessed February 18, 2015. www.nikkenfoods .com/products-page/sodium-reduction-pantry/komi-powder-7400/.

"New Formulation to Reduce Salt and Enhance Flavor in Soups." LycoRed Group, May 19, 2012. www.lycored.com/site/NewsEvents/News/News Expansion/tabid/95/ArticleId/10/New-formulation-to-Reduce -Salt-and-Enhance-Flavor-in-Soups.aspx.

Ohsu, Takeaki, et al. "Involvement of the Calcium-Sensing Receptor in Human Taste Perception." *Journal of Biological Chemistry* 285, no. 2 (January 8, 2010): 1016–22. doi:10.1074/jbc.M109.029165.

"A Role for Calcium in Taste Perception." EurekAlert!, January 8, 2010. www .eurekalert.org/pub_releases/2010-01/asfb-arf010810.php.

Ueda, Yoichi, et al. "Characteristic Flavor Constituents in Water Extract of Garlic." *Agricultural and Biological Chemistry* 54, no. 1 (January 1, 1990): 163–69. doi:10.1080/00021369.1990.10869909.

"Umami." *Wikipedia*. Accessed February 13, 2015. http://en.wikipedia.org/w /index.php?title=Umami&oldid=646899821.

LAZY FOODS

Rohrer, Finlo. "The Rise of Lazy Foods." *BBC News Magazine*, March 17, 2010.
http://news.bbc.co.uk/2/hi/uk_news/magazine/8572009.stm.

"Sales of 'Lazy Food' such as Pre-Sliced Fruit Increase." *Telegraph*, March 16,
2010. www.telegraph.co.uk/foodanddrink/foodanddrinknews/7448078
/Sales-of-lazy-food-such-as-pre-sliced-fruit-increase.html.

Thring, Oliver. "The Pre-Boiled Egg Marks the Beginning of the End." *Word of
Mouth* (blog), *Guardian*, July 9, 2009. www.theguardian.com/lifeandstyle
/wordofmouth/2009/jul/09/boiled-egg-happy.

LEXICAL-GUSTATORY SYNESTHESIA

McNeil, Donald G., Jr. "For Some, the Words Just Roll Off the Tongue." *New
York Times*, November 22, 2006. www.nytimes.com/2006/11/22
/science/23tastecnd.html.

Riley-Smith, Ben. "What Do London Underground Stops Taste Like?" *Telegraph*,
August 23, 2013. http://online-brokers.credio.com/w/7hPEunzQefr.

Ward, Jamie, and Julia Simner. "Lexical-Gustatory Synaesthesia: Linguistic
and Conceptual Factors." *Cognition* 89, no. 3 (October 2003): 237–61.
doi:10.1016/S0010-0277(03)00122-7.

LOCAPOUR

"Farm to Bar." Apothéke. Accessed March 30, 2015. www.apothekenyc.com/farm
-bar.

Friedman, Jesse. "SF Beer Week 2014 Special Releases." Almanac Beer Company,
January 8, 2014. www.almanacbeer.com/2014/01/sfbw2014-releases/.

Garris, Amanda. "Economists Explore 'Loca-Pouring' of Wines." *Cornell Chronicle*,
October 15, 2003. www.news.cornell.edu/stories/2013/10/economists
-explore-loca-pouring-wines.

"The Virtues and Pleasures of Being a 'Locapour.'" *Globe and Mail*, September
13, 2008. www.theglobeandmail.com/life/the-virtues-and-pleasures-of
-being-a-locapour/article716025/.

MEATMARE

Dickens, Charles. *A Christmas Carol and Other Christmas Writings*. Edited by
Michael Slater. London: Penguin Classics, 2003.

John Ward's Electric Séance, Vol. 1. Accessed February 18, 2015. http://johnward
.bandcamp.com/album/john-wards-electric-s-ance-vol-1.

"MeatMares and Meat Sweats." *Epic Meal Time*. Accessed March 27, 2015. www
.epicmealtime.com/2013/01/21/meatmares-and-meat-sweats/.

SunGazingVegan. "Have You Ever Had a Dream about Eating Meat?" Veggieboards,

May 12, 2009. www.veggieboards.com/forum/11-vegetarian-support
forum/97730-have-you-ever-had-dream-about-eating-meat-meatmares
.html#post2263199.

"The Quicksilver Meat Dream." *Wikipedia*. Accessed May 9, 2014. http://
en.wikipedia.org/w/index.php?title=The_Quicksilver_Meat_Dream
&oldid=607712571.

MEAT STYLUS

Golijan, Rosa. "Sausage Stylus Review: A Surprisingly Useful iPad Accessory."
Gizmodo, May 25, 2010. http://gizmodo.com/5547547/sausage-stylus
-review-a-surprisingly-useful-ipad-accessory.

"Mini Sausage on the iPhone Craze [translation]." *inews24*, February 9, 2010.
http://news.inews24.com/php/news_view.php?g_serial=474508&g
_menu=022600.

Patel, Nilay. "South Korean iPhone Users Turn to Sausages as a Cold Weather 'Meat
Stylus.'" *Engadget*, February 11, 2010. www.engadget.com/2010/02/11
/south-korean-iphone-users-turn-to-sausages-as-a-cold-weather-me/.

"Sumaho Corresponding Sausage Gloves [translation]." Daily Portal Z, December
11, 2013. http://portal.nifty.com/kiji/131210162624_1.htm.

MINI COWS

Brasch, Sam. "6 Ways to Fight the Menace of Cow Burps." *Modern Farmer*, January 7,
2014. http://modernfarmer.com/2014/01/6-ways-to-fight-the-menace
-of-cow-burps/.

"Don't Have a Back 40? Try Mini-Cattle." MSNBC.com, January 3, 2006. www
.nbcnews.com/id/10697287/ns/business-us_business/t/dont-have
-back-try-mini-cattle/.

Fritsch, Peter, and Jose De Cordoba. "Udderly Fantastic: Cuba Hopes To Clone
Its Famous Milk Cow." *Wall Street Journal*, May 21, 2002. www.wsj.com
/articles/SB1021927734453270880.

Griepentrog, Troy. "Raise Small-Breed Milk Cows." *Mother Earth News*, August
3, 2009. www.motherearthnews.com/homesteading-and-livestock/small
-breed-milk-cows.aspx.

International Miniature Cattle Breeds Registry. Accessed February 19, 2015. www
.minicattle.com/.

Seal, Rebecca. "Why Mini Cows Could Save the Planet." *Guardian*, July 25, 2010.
www.theguardian.com/environment/2010/jul/25/miniature-cattle
-environmentally-friendly-beef.

MISOPHONIA

Bethea, Charles. "The Chewing Sound and the Fury." *New Republic*, July 18, 2013. www.newrepublic.com/article/113667/misophonia-treatment-what-if -chewing-sounds-ruined-your-life.

"Misophonia." *Wikipedia*. Accessed February 13, 2015. http://en.wikipedia .org/w/index.php?title=Misophonia&oldid=646972502.

"Misophonia: Kelly Ripa Has Rare Disorder." ABC News video. Accessed February 19, 2015. http://abcnews.go.com/2020/video/ripa-kelly -misophonia-medical-mystery-disorder-mental-health-2020-16383771.

"Symptoms and Triggers." Misophonia Online. Accessed February 19, 2015. www .misophonia.com/symptoms-triggers/.

Tauber, Alejandro. "The Horrible Anger You Feel at Hearing Someone Chewing Is Called Misophonia." *Motherboard*, September 13, 2014. http:// motherboard.vice.com/read/the-horrible-anger-you-feel-at-hearing -someone-chewing-is-called-misophonia.

MOM WINES

Hoffman, Jan. "A Heroine of Cocktail Moms Sobers Up." *New York Times*, August 14, 2009. www.nytimes.com/2009/08/16/fashion/16drunk.html.

Mad Housewife Cellars. Accessed March 31, 2015. www.madhousewifecellars .com/wines/.

Stampler, Laura. "Wine Increasingly Marketed To Moms." *Huffington Post*, June 16, 2011. www.huffingtonpost.com/2011/06/16/mommy-themed-wines-meet -r_n_878220.html.

Walsh, Danielle. "Reinventing Mom Wine: Pinot Grigio, White Zin Redeemed!" *Bon Appétit*, May 29, 2014. www.bonappetit.com/drinks/wine/article /mom-wine.

"Wine for Mommy Sets off Trademark Fight." Reuters. April 20, 2011. www.reuters .com/article/2011/04/21/us-wine-mommy-idUSTRE73J80920110421.

NANOBREWERY

French, Matt. "Introducing the Nano-Magic." *Brew Magic Blog*, May 8, 2012. www .brewmagic.com/blog/nano-magic-by-sabco-2-bbl-rims-brewhouse/.

Garrison, Mark. "Pint Sized." *Slate*, December 12, 2012. www.slate.com/articles /business/drink/2012/12/nanobrewing_how_tiny_beer_making _operations_are_changing_the_industry.html.

Skubic, Michael. "The Great Nanobrewery List: From CA to MA." *Hess Brewing Odyssey* (blog), December 30, 2012. http://hessbrewing.blogspot .com/2009/11/nanobreweries-in-usa.html.

NOMMUNICATION

Alecci, Scilla. "Japan: Drinkommunication, When Drinking Alcohol Is a Social Obligation." *Global Voices*, September 12, 2010. http://globalvoicesonline .org/2010/09/12/japan-drinkommunication-when-drinking-alcohol-is -a-social-obligation/.

"Global Status Report on Alcohol and Health 2014." World Health Organization. Accessed February 19, 2015. www.who.int/substance_abuse/publications /global_alcohol_report/en/.

Kopp, Rochelle. "Nommunication—The Japanese Truth Serum." Japan Intercultural Consulting, January 3, 2013. www.japanintercultural.com /en/news/?newsID=235.

Sekiguchi, Toko. "Japan Inc. Is Drinking Again." *Time*, September 6, 2007. http:// content.time.com/time/magazine/article/0,9171,1659719,00.html.

"What Ales You: Your New Neighborhood Japanese-Beer Bar." UrbanDaddy, October 5, 2009. www.urbandaddy.com/la/nightlife/7396/Salaryman_Your _New_Neighborhood_Japanese_Beer_Bar_Los_Angeles_LA_Los_Feliz_Bar.

World Health Organization, "WHO Calls On Governments to Do More to Prevent Alcohol-Related Deaths and Diseases," news release, May 12, 2014. www.who.int/mediacentre/news/releases/2014/alcohol-related -deaths-prevention/en/.

NUT RAGE

DeCiantis, Devin, and Ivan Lansberg. "A Little Nut Rage Is Good." *Atlantic*, March 13, 2015. www.theatlantic.com/international/archive/2015/03/a-little -nut-rage-is-good/387787/.

Eun-Jee, Park. "Uproar Prompts Koreans to Buy Macadamia Nuts." *Korea JoongAng Daily*, December 13, 2014. http://koreajoongangdaily.joins .com/news/article/article.aspx?aid=2998466.

Nam, In-Soo. "Korean Air Executive Ejects Crew Member After Poor Nut Service." *Korea Real Time* (blog), *Wall Street Journal*, December 8, 2014. http://blogs.wsj.com/korearealtime/2014/12/08/korean-air-executive -ejects-crew-member-after-poor-nut-service/.

"'Nut Rage' Trial: Korean Air Executive Treated Crew 'like Slaves.'" *Guardian*, February 2, 2015. www.theguardian.com/world/2015/feb/02/nut-rage -trial-korean-air-lines-cho-hyun-ah.

Park, Madison, and Paula Hancocks. "Korean Air Executive Jailed over 'Nut Rage' Incident." CNN, February 12, 2015. www.cnn.com/2015/02/12/world /asia/korean-air-nut-rage-verdict/index.html.

"South Korea 'Nut Rage' Executive Heather Cho Freed." BBC News, May 22, 2015. www.bbc.com/news/world-asia-32840725.

Taylor, Adam. "Why 'Nut Rage' Is Such a Big Deal in South Korea." *Washington Post*, December 12, 2014. www.washingtonpost.com/blogs/worldviews/wp/2014/12/12/why-nut-gate-is-such-a-big-deal-in-south-korea/.

NUTRICOSMETICS

Global Industry Analysts, Inc. "Nutricosmetics—A Global Strategic Business Report." February 25, 2015. www.strategyr.com/pressMCP-6498.asp.

Rosenbloom, Stephanie. "Cosmetics That You Eat or Drink." *New York Times*, December 14, 2011. www.nytimes.com/2011/12/15/fashion/cosmetics-that-you-eat-or-drink.html.

Simpson, Paula. "A Fresh Look at Nutricosmetics: Where Are We Now?" *Nutraceuticals World*, September 2, 2013. www.nutraceuticalsworld.com/issues/Beauty-IO-2013/view_features/a-fresh-look-at-nutricosmetics-where-are-we-now/.

Starling, Shane. "Beauty Yoghurt Turns Ugly for Danone." NutraIngredients, February 6, 2009. www.nutraingredients.com/Manufacturers/Beauty-yoghurt-turns-ugly-for-Danone.

ORTHOREXIA NERVOSA

Bratman, Steven, and David Knight. *Health Food Junkies: Orthorexia Nervosa: Overcoming the Obsession with Healthful Eating.* New York: Broadway, 2001.

Donini, L. M., et al. "Orthorexia Nervosa: Validation of a Diagnosis Questionnaire." *Eating and Weight Disorders—Studies on Anorexia, Bulimia and Obesity* 10, no. 2 (2005): e28–32.

Grose, Sarah Horne. "10 Ways to Recognize Orthorexia." *The Cut* (blog), *New York*, July 17, 2014. http://thecutsocial.nymag.com/thecut/2014/07/10-ways-to-spot-an-orthorexic.html.

"Orthorexia Nervosa." *Wikipedia.* Accessed February 6, 2015. http://en.wikipedia.org/w/index.php?title=Orthorexia_nervosa&oldid=645866152.

Pfeffer, Stephanie Emma. "Popular Food Blogger—the Blonde Vegan—Admits to Eating Disorder." *People*, July 15, 2014. www.people.com/article/blonde-vegan-jordan-younger-blogger-eating-disorder-orthorexia.

Younger, Jordan. "Why I'm Transitioning Away from Veganism…" *Balanced Blonde* (blog), June 23, 2014. www.theblondevegan.com/2014/06/23/why-im-transitioning-away-from-veganism/.

PASSIVE DRINKING

Burgess, Adam. "'Passive Drinking': A 'Good Lie' Too Far?" *Health, Risk & Society* 11, no. 6 (December 1, 2009): 527–40. doi:10.1080/13698570903329482.

Donaldson, Liam. *150 Years of the Annual Report of the Chief Medical Officer: On the State of Public Health 2008*. Department of Health, United Kingdom, March 16, 2009. https://workspace.imperial.ac.uk/ref/Public/UoA%2001%20%20Clinical%20Medicine/CMO%20annual%20report.pdf#page=15.

Quinion, Michael. "Passive Drinking." World Wide Words. Accessed February 19, 2015. www.worldwidewords.org/turnsofphrase/tp-pas2.htm.

Smith, Rebecca. "'Passive Drinking' Is Blighting the Nation, Sir Liam Donaldson Warns." *Telegraph*, March 16, 2009. www.telegraph.co.uk/news/health/news/5000433/Passive-drinking-is-blighting-the-nation-Sir-Liam-Donaldson-warns.html.

POT WINE

Bienenstock, David. "I Drank Melissa Etheridge's Weed-Infused Wine." MUNCHIES, November 11, 2014. http://munchies.vice.com/articles/i-drank-melissa-etheridges-weed-infused-wine.

Kronsberg, Matthew. "Beyond Pot Brownies." *Gourmet Live*, October 5, 2011. www.gourmet.com/food/gourmetlive/2011/100511/beyond-pot-brownies.

Shallow, Parvati. "Cannabis-Infused Wine Delivers a 'Full Body Buzz' Says Melissa Etheridge." CBS News, December 3, 2014. www.cbsnews.com/news/cannabis-infused-wine-delivers-a-full-body-buzz-says-melissa-etheridge/.

Steinberger, Michael. "Marijuana-Laced Wine Grows More Fashionable in California Wine Country." *Daily Beast*, April 14, 2012. www.thedailybeast.com/articles/2012/04/14/marijuana-laced-wine-grows-more-fashionable-in-california-wine-country.html.

PREGOREXIA

Abraham, Laurie. "The Perfect Little Bump." *New York*, September 27, 2004. http://nymag.com/nymetro/health/features/9909/.

Brys, Shannon. "New Web-Based Support Group for Pregnant Women and Moms with Eating Disorders." Addiction Professional, February 18, 2014. www.addictionpro.com/news-item/new-web-based-support-group-pregnant-women-and-moms-eating-disorders.

"I'm Pregnant and Anorexic." *Sun*, October 11, 2007. www.thesun.co.uk/sol/homepage/woman/real_life/314257/Pregorexic-Pregnant-but-anorexic-real-life.html.

Wallace, Kelly. "'Pregorexia': Extreme Dieting While Pregnant." CNN, November 20, 2013. www.cnn.com/2013/11/20/living/pregnant-dieting-pregorexia-moms/index.html.

RAOTA

Bennett, Colette. "Otaku: Is It a Dirty Word?" *Geek Out!* (blog), September 12, 2011. http://geekout.blogs.cnn.com/2011/09/12/otaku-is-it-a-dirty-word/.

Chang, David. "The State of Ramen: Dave Chang." Lucky Peach, January 12, 2015. http://luckypeach.com/the-state-of-ramen-david-chang/.

Lyon, Shire. "Ramen Noodles: A High-Class Makeover." *FG Magazine.* Accessed February 19, 2015. www.thefashionglobe.com/ramen-noodles.

Otaku South. Accessed February 19, 2015. www.otakusouth.com/.

RAOTA. Accessed February 19, 2015. www.raota.org/.

RECESSIPES

"Clara Cannucciari." *Wikipedia.* Accessed August 10, 2014. http://en.wikipedia.org/w/index.php?title=Clara_Cannucciari&oldid=620607966.

Great Depression Cooking with Clara. Accessed March 28, 2015. www.greatdepressioncooking.com.

Martin, Andrew. "Spam Turns Serious and Hormel Turns Out More." *New York Times,* November 14, 2008. www.nytimes.com/2008/11/15/business/15spam.html.

"The Recession of 2007–2009: BLS Spotlight on Statistics." United States Department of Labor: Bureau Of Labor Statistics, February 2012. www.bls.gov/spotlight/2012/recession/.

Recessipes: Recess(ion Rec)ipes, February 5, 2009. http://recessipes.blogspot.com/.

Singer, Natasha. "A Label for a Pleather Economy." *New York Times,* October 24, 2008. www.nytimes.com/2008/10/26/fashion/26words.html.

"10 Meals for $10 or Less." CNN, February 6, 2009. http://edition.cnn.com/2009/LIVING/02/06/recession.recipes.irpt/index.html.

SAFETY WINE

Darke, Robin. "Doomsday Preppers #11: Defending Against China with Homemade Pipe Bombs." *Sabotage Times,* November 19, 2012. http://sabotagetimes.com/reportage/doomsday-preppers-11-defending-against-china-with-homemade-explosives/.

Raber, Margaret. "Can Opening a Sparkling Wine Be Dangerous?" *Wine Spectator,* March 3, 2011. www.winespectator.com/webfeature/show/id/44559.

Teague, Lettie. "A 'Safety Wine' Around the World." *Wall Street Journal,* August 21, 2010. www.wsj.com/articles/SB10001424052748704868604575433813926707960.

Yarrow, Alder. "2004 Château du Rouët 'Cuvée Belle Poule' Blanc, Cotes de Provence, France." *Vinography,* May 21, 2008. www.vinography.com/archives/2008/05/2004_chateau_du_rouet_cuvee_be.html.

SELMELIER

Bitterman, Mark. "An Encomium to Salt." *Salt News*, July 24, 2006. www.saltnews
.com/2006/07/an-encomium-to-salt/.

_____. *Salted: A Manifesto on the World's Most Essential Mineral, with Recipes.*
New York: Clarkson Potter/Ten Speed/Harmony, 2010.

Quinion, Michael. "Selmelier." World Wide Words. Accessed February 19, 2015.
www.worldwidewords.org/weirdwords/ww-sel1.htm.

SHEDISTA

Garagista Group. Accessed February 19, 2015. www.garagistagroup.com/.

Lawther, James. "Bordeaux: Calling Time on Garage Wine." *Decanter*, April 11, 2008.
www.decanter.com/people-and-places/wine-articles/485874/bordeaux
-calling-time-on-garage-wine.

McInerney, Jay. *A Hedonist in the Cellar: Adventures in Wine.* London: A&C Black,
2012.

Prinzing, Debra. "Are You a SHEDISTA?" *Debra Prinzing* (blog), December 11,
2008. www.debraprinzing.com/2008/12/11/are-you-a-shedista/.

SHMEAT

BiteLabs. Accessed February 19, 2015. http://bitelabs.org.

Churchill, Winston. "Fifty Years Hence." Teaching American History. http://
teachingamericanhistory.org/library/document/fifty-years-hence/.

Fountain, Henry. "A Lab-Grown Burger Gets a Taste Test." *New York Times*,
August 5, 2013. www.nytimes.com/2013/08/06/science/a-lab-grown
-burger-gets-a-taste-test.html.

Merchant, Brian. "The Guy Who Wants to Sell Lab-Grown Salami Made of
Kanye West Is '100% Serious.'" *Motherboard*, February 26, 2014. http://
motherboard.vice.com/read/the-guy-who-want-to-sell-you-salami
-made-out-of-james-franco-are-100-serious.

SMUSHI

Carlson, David. "The Royal Café Goes to Tokyo." *David Report* (blog), October 15,
2010. http://davidreport.com/201010/the-royal-cafe-goes-to-tokyo/.

Danish Minies. Accessed February 19, 2015. http://danishmini.dk/forside.

Maxwell, Kerry. "Smushi." *Macmillan Online Dictionary*, August 4, 2008. www
.macmillandictionary.com/us/buzzword/entries/smushi.html.

Schroeder, Katrina, and Carol Schroeder. "Smørrebrød in Miniature." *Eat Smart
in Denmark* (blog), November 27, 2013. http://blogs.denmark.dk
/eatsmart/2013/11/27/smorrebrod-in-miniature/.

"Smørrebrød 2.0." Denmark. Accessed March 31, 2015. http://denmark.dk/en /lifestyle/food-drink/smoerrebroed/.

"Yo Smushi." *Monocle*, November 2007. http://monocle.com/film/design/yo -smushi/.

SNACKIFY

Akst, Daniel. "The Snackification of Everything." *Los Angeles Times*, December 19, 2014. www.latimes.com/opinion/op-ed/la-oe-akst-snacks-20141221 -story.html.

Bauerlein, Valerie. "PepsiCo's Latest Challenge: 'Snackify' Some Beverages." *Wall Street Journal*, December 28, 2010. www.wsj.com/articles/SB100014240 52970204467204576047900383643010.

Clements, Warren. "Word Play: It May Simplify, but Should We Dignify Snackify?" *Globe and Mail*, February 4, 2011. www.theglobeandmail .com/arts/word-play-it-may-simplify-but-should-we-dignify-snackify /article622060/.

"Thought for Food—Fruit Pouch, Doritos Ad & Super Big Gulp." *Colbert Report* video, 8:21. First broadcast January 13, 2011, by Comedy Central. http://thecolbertreport.cc.com/videos/nhx7bu/thought-for-food---fruit -pouch--doritos-ad---super-big-gulp.

SNACKWAVE

Cills, Hazel, and Gabrielle Noone. "Snackwave: A Comprehensive Guide To The Internet's Saltiest Meme." *Hairpin*, September 15, 2014. http:// thehairpin.com/2014/09/snackwave-a-comprehensive guide-to-the -internets-saltiest-meme/.

Ilyas, Sara. "Jeremy Scott's Debut Runway Collection for Moschino—in Pictures." *Guardian*, February 21, 2014. www.theguardian.com/fashion /gallery/2014/feb/21/jeremy-scotts-debut-runway-collection-moschino -pictures-spongebob-squarepants.

SOMEWHERENESS

Deeping, Warwick. *Old Pybus*. New York: A. A. Knopf, 1928.

Kramer, Matt. *Making Sense of California Wine*. New York: William Morrow & Co, 1992.

Somewhereness. Accessed February 19, 2015. www.somewhereness.com/.

"SOMEWHERENESS—Reviews & Brand Information—Charles Baker Wines Toronto, Ontario, Serial Number: 85260007." Accessed February 19, 2015. www.trademarkia.com/somewhereness-85260007.html.

SOURDOUGH HOTEL

Alford, Henry. "Stockholm, and the Strangers Who Brought Me There." *New York Times*, June 15, 2012. www.nytimes.com/2012/06/17/travel/stockholm -and-the-strangers-who-brought-me-there.html.

Matray, Margaret. "Newcastle Woman Maintains 122-Year-Old Sourdough Starter." *Casper Star-Tribune Online*, December 4, 2011. http://trib .com/news/state-and-regional/newcastle-woman-maintains--year-old -sourdough-starter/article_000fcb17-5a5a-5590-84c2-3b55bb1d80fa.html.

Rothschild, Nathalie. "The Sourdough Hotel: A Cultural Centre." *Word of Mouth* (blog), *Guardian*, May 30, 2012. www.theguardian.com/lifeandstyle /wordofmouth/2012/may/30/the-sourdough-hotel-cultural-centre.

"Sourdough." *Wikipedia*. Accessed February 19, 2015. http://en.wikipedia.org/w /index.php?title=Sourdough&oldid=647792942.

Urban Deli. Accessed February 19, 2015. www.urbandeli.org/hem/.

Vail, Sharon. "Sourdough: More than a Bread." *Kitchen Window*, September 12, 2006. www.npr.org/templates/story/story.php?storyId=6061648.

SPOOFULATED

Asimov, Eric. "The Big Question: What's in Wine?" *New York Times*, May 30, 2013. www.nytimes.com/2013/06/05/dining/the-big-question-whats -in-wine.html.

Czerwinski, Joe. "Natural Wine or Unnatural Beverage." *Wine Enthusiast*, May 2010. www.winemag.com/May-2010/Natural-Wine-or-Unnatural-Beverage/.

Guerra, Sue. "And the Winner Is: Spoofulation." *On the Vine* (blog), *New Jersey Monthly*, March 11, 2010. http://njmonthly.com/blogs/on-the -vine/2010/3/11/and-the-winner-is-spoofulation.html.

Lefevere, Jeff. "2007 Dictionary New Word Entry Nominee: Spoofulate." *Good Grape: A Wine Blog Manifesto*, September 17, 2007. http://goodgrape .com/index.php/articles/comments/2007_dictionary_new_word_entries/.

Teague, Lettie. "The Actual Facts Behind the Rise of Natural Wine." *Wall Street Journal*, July 11, 2013. www.wsj.com/articles/SB100014241278873244 36104578579650208883968.

TRIGGER FOODS

Hanks, Andrew S., David R. Just, and Brian Wansink. "Trigger Foods: The Influence of 'Irrelevant' Alternatives in School Lunchrooms." *Agricultural and Resource Economics Review* 41, no. 1 (April 2012). http://papers.ssrn .com/sol3/papers.cfm?abstract_id=2016432.

Just, David R., and Brian Wansink. "Smarter Lunchrooms: Using Behavioral Economics to Improve Meal Selection." *Choices* 24, no. 3 (2009): 1–7.

TWECIPES

Downes, Lawrence. "Take 1 Recipe, Mince, Reduce, Serve." *New York Times*, April 22, 2009. www.nytimes.com/2009/04/22/dining/22twit.html.

Evans, Maureen. *Eat Tweet: 1,020 Recipe Gems from the Twitter Community's @ cookbook.* New York: Artisan, 2010.

Jamieson, Ruth, and Morwenna Ferrier. "Stuck for a Recipe? Just Use Twitter and Find a Top Chef." *Guardian*, March 28, 2009. www.theguardian.com /lifeandstyle/2009/mar/29/twitter-recipes.

Twitter @cookbook Glossary. Accessed May 20, 2015. http://cookbookglossary .pbworks.com/w/page/9614902/FrontPage.

UGLY FRUIT

Buerk, Roland. "Japan's Obsession with Perfect Fruit." BBC News. Accessed February 20, 2015. www.bbc.co.uk/news/world-radio-and-tv-17352173.

Fruta Feia. Accessed February 20, 2015. www.frutafeia.pt/.

Godov, Maria. "In Europe, Ugly Sells In The Produce Aisle." *The Salt* (blog), NPR, December 9, 2014. www.npr.org/blogs/thesalt/2014/12/09/369613561 /in-europe-ugly-sells-in-the-produce-aisle.

Mulholland, Rory. "'Ugly' Fruit and Vegetables Prove a Hit in France." *Telegraph*, September 30, 2014. www.telegraph.co.uk/news/worldnews/europe /france/11131994/Ugly-fruit-and-vegetables-prove-a-hit-in-France.html.

URGE SURFING

Jenkins, Kim T., and Katy Tapper. "Resisting Chocolate Temptation Using a Brief Mindfulness Strategy." *British Journal of Health Psychology* 19, no. 3 (September 2014): 509–22. doi:10.1111/bjhp.12050.

"Riding the Wave: Using Mindfulness to Help Cope with Urges." Portland Psychotherapy. Accessed February 20, 2015. www.portlandpsycho therapyclinic.com/counseling/blog/riding-wave-using-mindfulness-help -cope-urges.

Safer, Debra L., Christy F. Telch, and Eunice Y. Chen. *Dialectical Behavior Therapy for Binge Eating and Bulimia.* New York: Guilford Press, 2009.

"Surfing The Urge: G. Alan Marlatt on Mindfulness-Based Relapse Prevention." Inquiring Mind, 2010. www.inquiringmind.com/Articles /SurfingTheUrge.html.

VEGETABLE BUTCHER

Patronite, Rob, and Robin Raisfeld. "Eataly's Vegetable Butcher Revealed." *Grub Street* (blog), *New York*, August 18, 2010. www.grubstreet.com/2010/08 /eatalys_vegetable_butcher_reve.html.

Peraino, Anna. "Vegetarian Butcher Shop Open." *VegNews Daily*, January 10, 2011. www.vegetarianbutcher.com/.

Rainey, Clint. "America Is About to Get the World's First Vegan Butcher Shop." *Grub Street* (blog), *New York*, November 26, 2014. www.grubstreet.com/2014/11/vegan-butcher-shop.html.

"Siblings Build A Butcher Shop For 'Meat'-Loving Vegans." *The Salt* (blog), NPR, December 7, 2014. www.npr.org/blogs/thesalt/2014/12/07/369069078/siblings-build-a-butcher-shop-for-meat-loving-vegans.

VENDRIFICATION

Crowley, Chris E. "Feeding People and Communities One Year After Hurricane Sandy." *Serious Eats*, October 16, 2013. http://newyork.seriouseats.com/2013/10/lasting-relief-hurricane-sandy.html.

Flint Marx, Rebecca. "Turnarounds: How Food Trucks Went From 'Scourge' to 'Savior.'" *Grub Street* (blog), *New York*, November 19, 2012. www.grubstreet.com/2012/11/food-truck-image-reversal-after-sandy.html.

Robbins, Katie. "Vendrification: Street Food Streetfights." *BlackBook*, September 25, 2009. www.bbook.com/vendrification-street-food-streetfights/.

Simmons, Ann M. "Mobile Food Vendors Told to Leave Miracle Mile." *Los Angeles Times*, August 24, 2009. http://articles.latimes.com/2009/aug/24/local/me-wilshire-food-trucks24.

VINOTHERAPY

Caudalie: Natural Skin Care & Anti-Aging Treatments for All Skin Types. Accessed February 20, 2015. http://us.caudalie.com/.

Giles, Matthew. "Why Amar'e Stoudemire and a Bunch of Other Rich People Are Bathing in Red Wine." *Science of Us* (blog), *New York*, October 20, 2014. http://sousocial.nymag.com/scienceofus/2014/10/why-amare-stoudemire-is-bathing-in-red-wine.html.

Kerber, Fred. "Amar'e Stoudemire's New Physical Therapy: Red Wine Bath." *New York Post*, October 16, 2014. http://nypost.com/2014/10/16/amare-stoudemires-new-physical-therapy-red-wine-bath/.

"Vinotherapy Baths." Kenwood Inn and Spa. Accessed February 20, 2015. www.kenwoodinn.com/spa_bath_treatments.php.

VIRTUAL WATER

Allan, John Anthony. *Virtual Water: Tackling the Threat to Our Planet's Most Precious Resource*. New York: I. B.Tauris, 2011.

Malone, Bill, and Michael S. Davidow. "How 'Virtual Water' Can Help Ease California's Drought." *Wall Street Journal*, March 20, 2015. www.wsj.com

/articles/bill-davidow-and-michael-malone-how-virtual-water-can
-help-ease-californias-drought-1426891721.

"Scientist Who Invented 'Virtual Water' Wins Prize." Reuters, March 19, 2008.
www.reuters.com/article/2008/03/19/idUSL18502272.

*Virtual Water Trade: Proceedings of the International Expert Meeting on Virtual
Water Trade.* Research Report Series No. 12. IHE Delft, February 2003.
www.waterfootprint.org/Reports/Report12.pdf.

WALKAWAYS

Griffiths, Sarah. "Device for Supermarket Trolleys Could Cut Queue Times."
Daily Mail, February 11, 2015. www.dailymail.co.uk/sciencetech/article
-2949158/End-checkout-queue-Supermarket-trolley-GPS-cut-waiting
-times-guide-customers-special-offers.html.

Hauss, Debbie. "Queue Science Helps Retailers Recover Revenue at Checkout."
Retail TouchPoints, August 7, 2008. www.retailtouchpoints.com
/retail-store-ops/125-queue-science-helps-retailers-recover-revenue-at
-checkout.

Prigg, Richard. "Eliminating Customer Walk-Aways with Queue Science." RIS
Retail Info Systems News, September 23, 2008. http://risnews.edgl
.com/retail-news/Eliminating-Customer-Walk-Aways-with-Queue
-Science35886.

"Queueing Theory." *Wikipedia*. Accessed February 19, 2015. http://en.wikipedia
.org/w/index.php?title=Queueing_theory&oldid=647891837.

WHITE WHALE

Dawson, Patrick. "Tasting Ghost Whales." All About Beer, September 15, 2014.
http://allaboutbeer.com/article/ghost-whales/.

Locker, Melissa. "It's a Whale Of An Ale: Portland, Ore's Rogue Brewery Makes a
'Moby Dick' Flavored Beer." *Time*, November 23, 2012. http://newsfeed
.time.com/2012/11/23/its-a-whale-of-an-ale-portland-ores-rogue
-brewery-makes-a-moby-dick-flavored-beer/.

Perozzi, Christna. "Four Elusive 'White Whale' Beers That Are Still on the Loose."
Eater, February 20, 2015. www.eater.com/drinks/2015/2/20/8077349
/the-white-while-the-most-elusive-craft-beers.

"2014 Talkbeer.com Committee White Whale List." TalkBeer, February 23, 2014.
www.talkbeer.com/community/threads/2014-talkbeer-com-committee
-white-whale-list.6837/.

WINE APARTMENTS

Fujita, Junko. "Tokyo Developer Uncorks Apartment Building for Wine Lovers."
Reuters, October 1, 2013. www.reuters.com/article/2013/10/01/us
-japan-wine-apartment-idUSBRE99007Z20131001.

"Is Peyton Manning Becoming a Grapefriend?" Grapefriend (blog), September 5, 2012.
http://grapefriend.com/2012/09/05/is-peyton-manning-becoming
-a-grapefriend-broncos-shanahan/.

"Royal Champagne Hotel to Get The Caudalie Treatment." Wine-Searcher,
October 13, 2014. www.wine-searcher.com/m/2014/10/royal-champagne
-hotel-to-get-the-caudalie-treatment.

Wine Apartment. Accessed February 20, 2015. http://wineapartment.jp/en/.

WINE RAVE

Brown, Patricia Leigh. "Food Raves Gain in Popularity." New York Times, April 14,
2011. www.nytimes.com/2011/04/15/us/15rave.html.

Mangio, Frank. "Premier San Diego Wine & Food Festival Nov. 12-16." Coast
News, November 11, 2008. https://thecoastnews.com/blog/2008/11
/premier-san-diego-wine-food-festival-nov-12-16/.

Stevenson, Alison. "I Went to an LA Wine Rave." MUNCHIES, January 10, 2015.
https://munchies.vice.com/articles/the-wine-rave-is-a-state-of-mind.

Virbila, S. Irene. "Want to Go to a Wine Rave? Wine Cocktails. Glow Sticks." Los
Angeles Times, January 7, 2015. www.latimes.com/food/dailydish/la-dd
-wine-rave-honeycut-20150106-story.html.

ZIP CODE WINERY

Chamberlain, Lynn Krielow. "WineFairy Chats with Sergio Esposito, The Italian
Wine Merchant; and with Spring Mountain Man-Stu Smith of Smith-
Madrone." Vin de Cru (blog). Accessed February 20, 2015. http://
vinvillage.com/vin-de-cru/vvr-jul09-08.

Goodyear, Dana. "Drink Up: The Rise of Really Cheap Wine." New Yorker, May
18, 2009. www.newyorker.com/magazine/2009/05/18/drink-up.

"How to Read a Wine Label." Napa Valley Vintners. Accessed February 20, 2015.
www.napavintners.com/wines/how_to_read_a_wine_label.asp.

ACKNOWLEDGMENTS

Eatymology started in 2009 when I began collecting food neologisms on my blog, TheFoodSection.com, under the banner "The Dictionary of Modern Gastronomy." Grandiose? Yes. But also tongue in cheek, because the words I assembled tended toward the odd and unusual ones you find here.

Early inspiration for the book came from Ben Schott, whose *Miscellany* books I snapped up, and whose (now sadly defunct) *New York Times* blog *Schott's Vocab* I read religiously. On a couple of occasions, Schott threw me a (digital) bone by linking to a few of my words, which was truly a thrill.

My heartfelt thanks go to my agent, Sharon Bowers, who believed in this project from my very first email, and to my editor, Stephanie Bowen, for her enthusiasm, feedback, and insights throughout the writing process. I want to also thank associate editor Anna Michels and the whole team at Sourcebooks for seeing the potential in *Eatymology* to go from concept to book.

Last but not least, I would like to thank Jillian Rahn for the wonderful illustrations that appear throughout the book and made everything from *aporkalypse* to *wine rave* come to life!

ABOUT THE AUTHOR

Josh Friedland is an award-winning food writer and author and the creator of @RuthBourdain, a Twitter mash-up that won the first-ever James Beard Award for Humor. His work has appeared in the *New York Times*, the *Washington Post*, *Olive* (BBC), *Time Out New York*, Epicurious, Chow, and Tasting Table.

© Lisa Rayman Goldfarb